CHINESE SINGLE BROADSWORD

—A Primer of Basic Skills and Performance Routines for Practitioners

Compiled by: Xie Zhikui
Consultant: Zeng Weiqi
Translated by: John Moffett
Drawings by: Xie Zhikun
Photographs by: Zhan Feng

FOREIGN LANGUAGES PRESS   BEIJING

First Edition   1990

ISBN 7-119-00830-7
ISBN 0-8351-2254-9

Copyright 1990 by Foreign Languages Press, Beijing, China

Published by Foreign Languages Press
24 Baiwanzhuang Road, Beijing 100037, China

Printed by Foreign Languages Printing House
19 West Chegongzhuang Xilu, Beijing 100044, China

Distributed by China International Book Trading Corporation
21 Chegongzhuang Xilu, Beijing 100044, China
P.O. Box 399, Beijing, China

Printed in the People's Republic of China

INTRODUCTION

Wushu (martial atrs) is one of the precious cultural inheritances of the Chinese people. Weapons are a category of Wushu. Amongst them, the broadsword has been used as an implement for hunting, self-defense and warfare purposes since the earliest times. The manufacture of iron and the development of casting skills gave impetus to the importance of the broadsword in life and warfare and owing to its superiority of killing effectiveness over other weapons in battle, it became one of the earliest of common military weapons. With the development of society, the broadsword became an integral part not only of warfare, but also physical exercise, daily life, labour, and even attire. As a result, changes in the broadsword's shape and techniques of employment developed and improved a great deal, encompassing an increasingly wide variety of designs.

As warfare and Wushu techniques developed, the varieties of weapons increased, and the broadsword became an indispensable item amongst the traditional Chinese "Eighteen Military Weapons" and the "Eighteen Military Arts."

The broadsword category can basically be divided today into the long-handled and short-handled varieties. Each type of broadsword has its own variety of routines and techniques acccording to the different styles and schools. Owing to its widespread use and varied form,

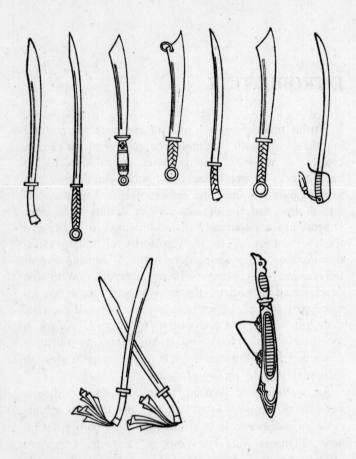

the broadsword has a large number of names, too numerous to mention here.

This book is intended to introduce a basic knowledge of the single broadsword, from simple-and-easy-to-learn routines up to the advanced-level routines mastered for performance and competition by the Wushu lover with

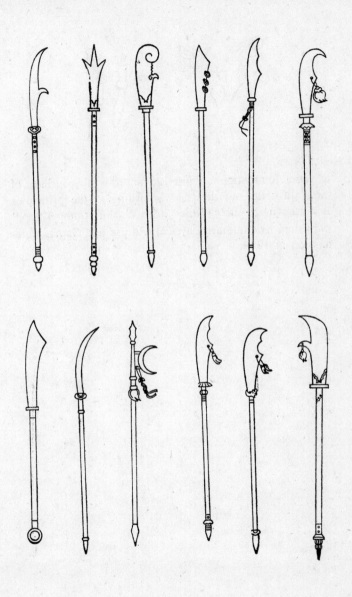

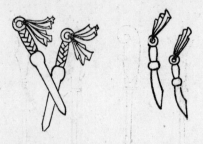

a good foundation. Those advanced-level routines of some difficulty are designed according to the principles laid down in the "Rules for Wushu Competition," published by the State Physical Culture and Sports Commission in 1979.

CONTENTS

Chapter I

REQUIRED KNOWLEDGE FOR THE PRACTICE OF THE SINGLE BROADSWORD

Section 1

GENERAL KNOWLEDGE ABOUT THE SINGLE BROADSWORD

1) The single broadsword belongs to the category of "short weapons." Its shape (Diag. A. 1) consists of seven parts, the body, point, blade, back, guard, hilt and base. The length of the body varies. For practice purposes it can be long or short, but for competition it must conform to the standard length as stipulated by competition regulations. The regulations state that the norm should be that when the sword is cradled in the straight arm, the point should not be below the performer's earlobe. A streamer made of silk may be attached as decoration to the base of the sword hilt, and this must not exceed the whole length of the sword. Following the changes of the character of broadsword routines in recent

Diag. A. 1

years, with an increasing trend towards speed and difficulty, the weight of the competition broadsword has gradually decreased. In the 1950's the broadsword weighed from more than 1 pound to over two; in the 1980's it weighs less than one pound. For the practice of the routines in this book, a light sword is best.

2) Can one practise broadsword if one has not already practised Wushu exercises? When practising Wushu one must first practise basic exercises and skills. After this one must practise a boxing skill routine. The practice of a weapon routine should be on the basis of mastery of such boxing skills. Weapon practice includes the easy and the difficult, usually first practising broadsword and staff, then rapier and lance. A Wushu saying goes, "A year for the lance, a month for the staff, a hundred days for the broadsword." This illustrates that each type of weapon has differing degrees of progress from the easy to the difficult in the process of practice. If one really wishes to master a specific weapon, it is best to progress gradually along the specified formal order of practice.

Why must one first practise basic skills, then boxing skills and finally weapon routines? This is because the basic skills are designed as preparation for the special techniques required for practice. In practising boxing skills one must master a certain number of technical movements and the required physical qualities. These technical movements and specialized physical qualities are those which must be thoroughly mastered for the practice of each class of weapon. The more correct and consolidated one's mastery of boxing movements, the more natural and thorough will be one's practice of weapon movements. For the convenience of the reader, this book reintroduces the specifications of some basic Wushu movements.

3) When first starting the practice of broadsword, one should first practise basic broadsword movements (that is broadsword basic skills). Through the practice of basic movements, one can gradually develop the strength of one's grip, increase the wrist's flexibility and grow accustomed to the fluctuations and use of the three gripping methods (full grip, half grip and pincer grip). Having mastered basic skills, one must repeatedly practise broadsword techniques according to their combat implications, knowing correctly the contact point and focus of force for each method; for instance, strength must reach the blade for a slice, so when practising one must lead with the mind causing the focus of force to reach the blade. Only with long practice will the focus of force be accurate, the strength full and solid. Other broadsword techniques must be practised in the same way. When one has fairly thoroughly mastered the basic skills and the focus of force and strength of several broadsword techniques one can then master the practice of the broadsword more easily.

Section 2

THE CHARACTERISTICS OF SINGLE BROADSWORD TECHNIQUES

Amongst Wushu weapons, the commonest of the short weapons are the broadsword and rapier. Their lengths are basically the same, but they differ considerably in technique characteristics and performance style.

1) The broadsword has a point, a back and a blade. The rapier has a point, blades but no back. Since both

have blade and point, many combat methods and results are the same. For instance, the broadsword has the Stab, Upward Thrust, Sweep Thrust, Side Press, Side Parry, Cut, Wave, etc., as does the rapier. But only the broadsword has a back, so it has certain distinct characteristics in its techniques and style. This is the crucial point in its distinction to the rapier. The most common movements in broadsword routines are "Entwining the Head" and "Binding the Head," and many others are the outcome of leading up to or going on from these two.

Why does the broadsword have these two movements and the rapier not? The completion of these movements strictly demands that the sword back sticks tightly to the torso as it traverses the back of the shoulders. This is appropriate since the broadsword does not have a bladed back. The rapier is bladed on both edges, so it is not appropriate to use this method, and were it to appear in a competition it would be seriously penalized.

2) Single broadsword is fast, powerful and ferocious in character. The sword-back has something to do with this, since the back, being fairly thick, increases the weight of the weapon, making it easier to apply strength during practice, facilitating the coordination of sword and strength, increasing the speed of the sword in movement and emphasizing its powerful character. Since its great speed during performance causes the sword and ribbon to make a rushing sound, its impact like the crashing of waves, this type of fast, powerful and simple style is a unique characteristic of the single broadsword. Hence the analogy, "The broadsword like a fierce tiger, the rapier like a roving dragon."

3) A common saying referring to different varieties of broadsword says: "For single broadsword watch the

hands, double-broadsword watch the footwork, big broadsword watch the lead hand." What does this "watch the hand" mean? When performing. one grasps the sword in one's right hand, the left following the various movements of the right in a series of differing hand movements involving degrees of arm extensions, swings, and palm forms. This serves to give the movements a unity of composition, greater balance, beauty and coordination. The general guidelines for the coordination of the left hand are: sword to the fore, left hand to the rear; sword to the left, left hand to the right; sword up, left hand down. There are also movements where both hands move in the same direction, for instance, Sword Push and Sword Press (where the left hand is usually in contact with the body of the sword). Thus, "watch the hands" means ensuring that the left hand to sword coordination is accurate and balanced, conforming to the principle of the left hand lending strength to the sword. It should be so that, when the sword moves, the left hand must move, when the hand moves the sword must move; the sword urges on the person's motion, the person urges on the swing of the sword. One must never have motion of sword with a static left hand, motion of the torso without motion of the legs, sword fast, left hand slow, torso fast, legs slow, etc. and other uncoordinated phenomena.

Section 3

THE BASIC ORDER OF SINGLE BROADSWORD ROUTINES FOR COMPETITION

The basic order for competition routines must include

the set groups of movements laid down in the "Rules for Wushu Competition" published by the State Physical Culture and Sports Commission in 1979.

Here is the list of specified contents for routines of the broadsword class.

A complete routine of the broadsword class must at least include the following:

1) The three main stances: Bow Stance, Crouching Stance, and Empty Stance.

2) It must include no less than eight different sets of sword technique. These must include the Slice, Sweep Thrust, Stab, Chop, Entwining the Head and Binding the Head.

3) Each type of leap and mid-air movement involving the execution of a sword technique should not appear more than twice, a spin not more than once.

4) Of the restricted tumble, pounce, roll and flip, only one may be chosen, which is only to be executed once and may be omitted.

5) A running leap or somersault may only be executed twice in the whole routine.

The competition routine in this book is compiled according to these regulations. The various hand methods, sword techniques, steps, stances and kicks included in them are as follows:

Stances:

Horse Stance	T-Stance
Bow Stance	Cross Stance
Crouching Stance	Side-Bow Stance
Rest Stance	Attention Stance
Empty Stance	Open Stance
Point Stance	

Footwork:
Arc Step
Striking Step
Forward Step
Retreating Step
Covering Step
Backward Insert Step

Leaping Step
Great Leaping Step
Kneeling Step
Stamp
Running Step

Kicks:
Spring Kick
Inward Kick

Side Kick
Splits

Leaps:
Flying Kick
Whirlwind Kick
Spin

Mid-air Side Roll
Leap

Balances:
Leg Hook Balance
Leaning Back Balance

Knee Raise Balance

Hand Forms:
Fist
Hook

Palm

Hand Techniques:
Palm Push
Exposed Palm
Supporting Palm
Slapping Palm

Palm Thrust
Palm Swing
Fist Raise
Hook

Sword Techniques:
Embracing
Back Rest
Concealing
Stab
Hack
Side Press
Parry

Side Parry
Upward Thrust
Jab
Swipe
Vertical Slash
Round the Middle Concealing
Entwining the Head

Press	Binding the Head
Chop	Wrist Shearing Flourish
Sweep Thrust	Upright Sword
Slice	Place
Push	Brandish
Wave	Throw
Cut	

Section 4

UNDERSTANDING THE DIAGRAMS AND DIRECTIONS

Only if one fully appreciates the diagrams will one be able to accurately teach oneself the movements. Hence, it is crucial to know how to interpret the diagrams and text.

1) The texts tend to use a great deal of specialist terminology, such as the various types of stance, footwork, etc. Before learning by oneself, one must first understand the whole process fixed in the content of a Wushu term. Otherwise one cannot accurately complete a technical move. All the technical terms used have explanations for your consultation.

2) The order of textual explanation is; first lower limb, footwork and stance, then upper limb, sword and hand techniques, and finally several important points to watch out for. Though the text is sequential, when completing a movement one must pay attention to the emphasis in the book on coordination between one part and another, and how the head and legs are coordinated. Only then will one complete a whole posture, and accurate and beautifully modelled movement.

3) Movement direction in the text is according to the position of the person and movement as placed in the diagrams. The overall arrangement of the advanced routine is fairly complex, the path of movement twisting and very variable. In order to ensure accuracy of route and direction, the directions of the footfall, chest and gaze are all indicated. Directional indications employ compass terms. The angle of revolution in a turn is explained or a line drawn from the waist, the arrow heads indicating the direction of the turn. One must study both the diagrams and the text, thus imitating the movement without any faults in direction or sequence.

4) Additional diagrams are sometimes inserted into the main diagram in order to illustrate a side or rear view of the posture.

5) The route of the lower and upper limb movements are indicated by the full line (→). The dotted line (-→) indicates the intended route of the part for the next movement, the tail of the arrow indicating the start, the head indicating the stopping point.

The parts indicated by the full and dotted lines are also:

Upper limbs: right arm, right hand, sword body (point, middle and hilt) are all indicated by full line (→); left arm, left hand and sword body by the dotted line (-→).

Lower limbs: Right foot is indicated by dotted line (-→); left foot by full line (→).

Waist: Swings of waist are shown by curved full line.

The direction of the sword movement should really be indicated from the tip of the blade, but for the sake of clarity and to fascilitate the distinguishing of the dotted and full lines the starting and stopping points of the lines

are drawn from the gripping hand or the sword body. Turns of the body are indicated by curved full lines.
Compass Directions in Diagrams:

From the Starting Posture, in front of the chest is South, behind the back is North, the left side is East, the right side West.

Section 5

TITLES AND DESCRIPTIONS OF BASIC HAND FORMS, STANCES, FOOTWORK, LEAPS, JUMPS AND ROLLS

1) Hand forms:

Fist	Hook
Palm	

2) Stances:

Bow Stance	Cross Stance
Horse Stance	Point Stance
Empty Stance	Side Bow Stance
Crouching Stance	Knee Raise Balance
Rest Stance	

3) Footwork:

Striking Step	Arc Step

4) Leaps:

Mid-air Kick	Whirlwind Kick

5) Jumps, rolls, etc. :

Back Drop
Carp Flips Erect
Black Dragon Entwining Pillar

Mid-air Side Spin	Spin

6) Explanation of terms used in this section

  1) **Hand Forms**

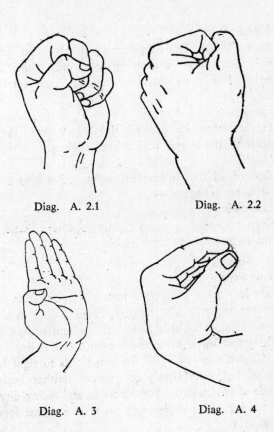

Diag. A. 2.1   Diag. A. 2.2

Diag. A. 3   Diag. A. 4

Fist:

Four fingers curled up together, thumb tightly pressed against the second joint of the fore and middle fingers. (Diag. A.2.1)

Essentials:

Fist must be tightly clenched (not half-clenched), fist face level, fist back, wrist and forearm forming a flat surface. (Diag. A. 2.2)

Palm:

Four fingers held together and extended straight, thumb bent and pressed tightly into the "Tiger's Mouth" (the part between thumb and forefinger). (Diag. A.3)

Essentials:

Fingers must be pressed tightly together, the bent knuckle of the thumb pulled back slightly.

Hook:

Tips of all five fingers pressed together into a point, wrist bent. (Diag. A.4)

Essentials:

Keep finger-tips pressed tightly together. Bend wrist as far as possible to form Hook.

2) Stances

Bow Stance:

Left foot takes a big step forward (about four or five times the person's foot length). Toes pulled in slightly (i.e. not dead straight ahead), left leg bent to half squat, thigh almost level, knee and toes in vertical line. Right leg straight, toes pulled in (so foot slants to right front), soles of both feet firmly on ground, neither heels nor outside of foot raised. Torso upright and facing direction of front leg. Fists pulled tight in to waist, gaze forward. (Diag. A.5)

Essentials:

Front leg bowed, almost to 90°. Back leg straight, chest out, sink waist, right hip pressing down. When left leg is forward this is a Left Bow Stance; when right leg is forward, a Right Bow Stance.

Easily made mistakes:

a) Raising heel or side of foot of back leg.

b) Bending waist so torso inclines forward.

Diag. A. 5

Corrective method:

a) Improve tendon flexibility of knee and ankle joints.

b) Emphasize straightness of back leg and heel forcibly pressing on floor.

c) Emphasize head pressing upward and hips pressing downward.

Horse Stance:

Open feet wide apart (about three times one's foot length), feet parallel and pointing forward. Legs bent to half squat, knees not protruding too far forward, thighs almost level. Soles of feet firmly on ground. Body's centre of gravity between two legs. Fists pulled tightly in to waist. (diag. A. 6.1)

Essentials:

Chest out, waist erect, head pressing upward, heels pressing outward, breathing natural.

Easily made mistakes:

a) Toes splaying outward, distance between feet too big or small.

b) Torso tilting forward, backside sticking out or

knees bent too much and kneeling forward.

Corrective methods:

a) Emphasize the toes pointing forward, heels pressing outward.

b) Be precise about width, measuring out the space between feet before practising Horse Stance.

c) Emphasize sticking out chest, erect waist and one's weight leaning back a little.

There is also a half Horse Stance, basically the same as the Horse Stance, but with the toes of one foot pointing outward. (Diag. A.6.2)

Diag. A. 6.1   Diag. A. 6.2

Empty Stance:

Feet apart front and back, left foot pointing outward at 45°, knee bent to half squat, right foot extended out to right front, knee slightly bent, toes pulled in a bit and just touching ground. Weight all on left leg, fists pulled in to waist, gaze forward. (Diag. A.7.1)

Essentials:

Chest out, waist erect, clear distribution of weight (empty and solid).

When the right foot is extended this is a Right Empty

Stance; when the left foot is extended a Left Empty Stance.

Easily made mistakes:

Indistinct weight distribution, centre shifting towards front leg, torso tilting forward.

Corrective methods:

a) Do not let the front foot touch the ground at first, waiting until one is firmly centred on the supporting leg before letting toes alight.

b) Practise squatting down on one leg to develop lower limb strength.

c) If one cannot manage the low Empty Stance at first, then one can practise with the supporting leg raised in the higher Empty Stance. (Diag. A. 7.2)

Diag. A. 7.1   Diag. A. 7.2

Crouching Stance:

Feet spread wide apart. Right knee bends to full squat, thigh and calf close together, buttocks close to lower leg, soles firmly on ground, toes and knee joints splayed slightly outward. Left leg stretched out to left side, toes pulled in (to face front), sole firmly on floor. Fists pulled

15

tightly in to waist, head turning left, gaze forward past left foot. (Diags. A.8.1, 2)

Diag. A. 8.1

Diag. A. 8.2

Essentials:

Chest out, waist erect, hips sunk. When left leg is extended this is a Left Crouching Stance; when right leg is extended, a Right Crouching Stance.

Easily made mistakes:

a) Extended leg not straight, outside of foot raised, toes raised or splayed outward.

b) The squatting leg not able to squat down properly, heel rising up, body tilting forward.

Corrective methods:

When spreading the legs, have the outside of one foot pressed up against a wall, squatting down fully on the other leg, then straightening up again. This will stretch the hip and ankle joints.

Rest Stance:

Stand upright with legs crossed, left forward, right behind, thighs pressed together. Then, bend knees to full squat, the right kneecap sticking out from behind the left leg and close to the outside of the left foot. Buttocks sit on right leg near the right heel. Left sole is firmly on ground, toes turned outward, right heel is raised. Fists pulled in tightly to waist, gaze forward. (Diags. A.9.1, 2)

Diag. A. 9.1   Diag. A. 9.2

Essentials:

Chest out, waist erect, two legs pressed firmly together, with body weight centred in between.

When the left leg is forward, this is a Left Rest Stance; when right leg is forward, a Right Rest Stance.

Easily made mistakes:

a) Legs not pressed firmly together.

b) Back leg's kneecap not poking out from behind front leg.

c) Front foot not turned outward, toes pointing forward instead.

Corrective methods:

a) Squat down after one has pressed the legs firmly together.

b) Emphasize the outward turn of front foot and back knee poking out.

T-Stance:

Stand erect with feet close together. Bend knees to half squat, right sole firmly on ground, left heel raised, toes touching ground beside right instep. Weight inclined onto right leg. Fists pulled in tightly to waist, gaze forward. (Diag. A.10)

Diag. A. 10

Essentials:

Chest out, waist erect, back side pulled in.

Easily made mistakes:

a) Torso tilting forward, backside stuck out.

b) Knees splayed apart.

c) Left toes not positioned accurately beside right instep.

Corrective methods:

Emphasize erect stance, backside pulled in, thighs pressed tightly together, left toes accurately placed.

Cross Stance:

Stand erect with right leg crossed behind left, thighs pressed close together, left knee bent forward, toes turned outward, sole pressed firmly on ground. Right leg is stretched out straight to left rear, heel raised. Fists pulled in tightly to waist. Gaze forward. For this stance bending right knee forward is also possible. (Diags. A. 11.1, 2)

Diag. A. 11.1   Diag. A. 11.2

Essentials:

Chest out, waist erect, back leg stretched out far, waist also twisted in line with front leg. When the left leg is forward, this is a Left Cross Stance; when the right leg is forward, a Right Cross Stance.

Easily made mistakes:

a) The feet too close together or the front-back distance too great.

b) Front knee not sufficiently bent, back leg not straight.

c) Torso tilted forward, waist not turned fully in line with front leg.

Corrective methods:

Emphasize the correct distance between feet, thighs close together, chest out and waist twisted.

Point Stance:

Right leg straight, toes turned outward a little. Left leg extended straight, foot stretched tight so toes touch ground in front of body. Fists pulled in tight to waist, gaze forward. (Diag. A.12 and Side View)

Diag. A. 12

Essentials:

Chest out, waist erect, both legs fully straight, weight inclined to rear. This stance is also sometimes called the High Empty Stance.

Easily made mistakes:

a) Front leg not straight, the body tilting backward as the weight inclines to the rear.

b) Not standing firm, the cause of which is the front

foot being in line with the back foot so the legs cross.

Corrective methods:

a) Press down with force with front foot toes.

b) Shift weight forward a little.

c) Emphasize the position of the left toes touching the ground, so they are a little to the left side. Avoid having left foot in line with right.

Side Bow Stance:

Stand erect with feet spread wide apart to left and right, toes pointing forward. Right knee bends to half squat, thigh almost level. Left leg straight, torso facing forward. Fists pulled in tightly to waist, gaze forward. (Diag. A.13)

Diag. A. 13

Essentials:

Chest out, waist erect, backside pulled in. When the right knee is bent this is a Right Side Bow Stance; when the left is bent, a Left Side Bow Stance.

Easily made mistakes:

a) Thigh not nearly level when knee is bent, too high or too low.

b) The outside of the extended leg's foot raised.

21

c) The toes of one or both feet turning outward.

d) Torso leaning forward or waist bent.

Corrective methods:

Emphasize that it is not the same as the Bow Stance, and improve flexibility of the ankle joints to avoid the raising of outside of foot.

Knee Raise Balance:

Stand firmly on right leg, torso erect, foot turned outward slightly. Bend and raise the left knee in front of body, till kneecap nears chest, lower leg pulled in tightly up against upper leg, the face of the foot stretched tight, ankle bent inward. Fists pulled in tight to waist. Gaze forward. (Diags. A.14.1, 2, Right and Left Knee Raise Balances.)

Essentials:

Chest out, waist erect, straight knee on supporting leg, bent-knee leg lifted high.

Easily made mistakes:

a) Supporting leg not straight, not standing steady.

b) Bent knee not high, lower leg not pulled in, hooked foot.

Corrective methods:

a) Improve flexibility of leg and hip joints.

b) Practise standing on one leg, raising the knee and holding the leg, alternating left and right. (Diag. A.14.3)

3) Footwork:

Striking Step:

a) Stand with feet apart front and back, supported by the right leg at back. Raise left leg preparing to step forward (East). Hands inserted at waist, gaze forward. (Diag. A.15.1)

b) Left foot lands forward, followed immediately by a leap forward from it. Right foot lifts off, both feet rising into the air, during which time the right instep moves forward to strike the left instep. (Diag. A.15.2)

c) After two feet have struck, right foot lands first. The left foot then lands in front of the body, gaze still forward. (Diag. A.15.3)

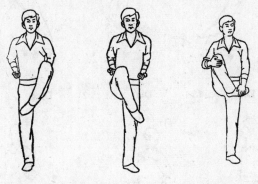

Diag. A. 14.1   Diag. A. 14.2   Diag. A. 14.3

Essentials:

While in mid-air one must maintain an erect torso, not leaning forward or back.

Arc Step:

a) Stand erect with left foot in front, right foot to rear, facing East. Fists pulled in tight to waist. (Diag. A.16.1)

b) Bend knees slightly, weight shifting forward. Right foot takes a step in an arc past left instep towards right front (S-E), toes turned outward as foot lands. Fists still at waist, gaze forward. (Diag. A.16.2)

c) Shift weight forward, left foot taking a step in an arc past right instep towards right front(S). Toes turn

Diag. A. 15.1   Diag. A. 15.2   Diag. A. 15.3

Diag. A. 16.1   Diag. A. 16.2   Diag. A. 16.3

inward as foot lands. Fists still at waist, gaze forward. (Diag. A.16.3)

Essentials:

Keep chest out, waist erect, legs maintaining their bent form. (Keep well centred and balanced.) Do not rise and fall as one steps forward. It is called an Arc Step because the path of progression is in an arc, the feet also moving in arcs when in mid-air. There is a Right Arc Step and a Left Arc Step, the difference being that the turning in or out of the feet on landing is opposite. There is no set number of paces for it, depending on the requirements of the movement, being sometimes more than ten, sometimes just a few. The Arc Step is one of the harder footwork skills and one can practise in a S form, moving left and right in continuous arcs of 10 or 20 metres back and forth.

4) Leaps

Mid-air Flying Kick:

a) Stand erect, feet together, facing East. Arms hang naturally at sides, gaze forward. First run forward(E) a couple of paces, raising left arm up to beside head, finishing with the right foot in front. Raise straight left leg up in front of body, leaping off from ground with right foot, so body soars into the air. At same time arms rise up and forward, right hand meeting left above the head in a slap. (Diags. A.17.1, 2, 3)

Diag. A. 17.1   Diag. A. 17.2

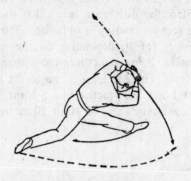

Diag. A. 17.3

b) Carry straight on. At the highest point in mid-air, kick forward and up with right leg, foot face stretched flat, slapping right foot face with right palm. At same time, left leg remains straight or bent below body, left palm at left side or at left front in hook form, hook point downward and slightly higher than shoulder. Gaze forward. (Diag. A.17.4 and Rear View)

Diag. A. 17.4

Rear View, Diag. A. 17.4

Essentials:

As the right leg spring-kicks forward, the foot should be higher than the waist, bent knee of left leg restrained in front of torso. The strike of the foot face should be crisp and accurate.

Easily made mistakes:

a) Inaccurate slap of foot face.

b) Inability to slap clearly in mid-air.

c) Inability to keep bent left knee in front of torso in mid-air.

Corrective methods:

a) Practise leaping from the right foot at a run, with simultaneous bending of left knee and slapping of hands.

b) Practise simple kicking and slapping of foot without leaping.

c) Increase practice of right foot springing power.

Whirlwind Kick:

a) Stand erect, both legs straight, weight supported on right leg, left foot to front(S), toes pointed and touching ground. Torso turned a little to left. Right palm raised up above head, fingers pointing to left. Left palm raised straight out to left side, fingers pointing up. Head turned to left, gaze forward. (Diag. A.18.1)

b) Left foot takes a step to left(E), leg slightly bent. Right leg stretches straight, heel rises, right arm moves down so that arms now are level at sides of body. Gaze in direction of left palm. (Diag. A.18.2)

c) Right foot takes a step forward(E), landing with toes pointing in (N), knee bent, the ball of the foot treading down with force. Left arm moves down, bending at elbow and brought in in front of right chest. Right arm moves up. Torso turns a little to left. (Diag. A.18.3)

Diag. A. 18.1   Diag. A. 18.2   Diag. A. 18.3

d) Carry straight on. Jump up from the right foot, both feet soaring into the air, body spinning round left and up. At same time, raise left leg either bent or straight towards upper left. Arms move down, then swing towards upper left. In this way the body spins right round leftwards. While turning, the right leg swings up and to inside left in an Inward Kick, sole turned inward, so that when the body has turned 270° the left palm comes down from above to meet the sole of the right foot in a slap. Left leg is bent at knee or naturally extended, the right arm swinging naturally at right side. (Diags. A.18.4, 5.)

Diag. A. 18.4   Diag. A. 18.5

Essentials:

The arm swing, leap, turn and kick must all be continuous and coordinated. The slap must be precise and crisp, executed while the left leg is still in mid-air. It is not easy for beginners to soar well into the air, but the sequence of the movement must be accurate and faultless.

Easily made mistakes:

a) Disjointed movement, insufficient angle of turn, slap not while air-bound.

b) After having jumped, the waist bends forward, the backside sinks or the torso tilts backward.

Corrective methods:

a) Practise swinging the left leg, Inward Kick with right leg and body spin on the ground.

b) Practise the take off and 360° mid-air spin with

arm swing without adding the kick, emphasizing erect torso and suspended head while spinning.

5) Jumps, Rolls, Etc.

Back Drop:

a) Stand erect, feet together, facing East. Arms hanging naturally at sides, gaze forward. (Diag. A.19.1)

Diag. A. 19.1

b) Right foot steps forward (E), immediately launching off from it, not too high, torso tilting and bending forward, head tucked in and body curled up. Arms are bent at elbows in front of chest. Left leg swings over from behind. (Diag. A.19.2)

c) Right shoulder lands first, followed by back of right side, waist and backside, rolling over in succession. Legs bent at knees, left foot behind right knee following forward movement of roll. (Diag. A.19.3)

Essentials:

One is not required to seek to soar in mid-air for the

Diag. A. 19.2

Diag. A. 19.3

Back Drop, the roll being quick and round. When one finishes, roll back onto one's feet, right foot in front of left.

Easily made mistakes:

a) Body not sufficiently curled up, roll not rounded.

Diag. A. 20.1

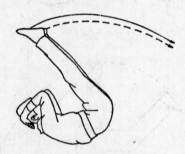

Supplementary diag.

b) Momentum not sufficient, the roll slow, standing up delayed.

c) Landing order incorrect, forming straight forward roll or side roll.

Corrective methods:

a) First practise forward rolls, to get the feel of tucking in the head, curling up the body, bending knees, doing fast rolls and standing up.

b) Emphasize right shoulder hitting ground first, tucking bent right arm in towards the left armpit, turning head a little to left as one tucks it in.

c) The Back Drop includes a mid-air and non mid-air Back Drop. The first must only be practised on the basis of the second.

Carp Flips Erect:

Lie on one's back. Swing legs up, folding body so that feet pass above head, hands support thighs, fingers facing, or are placed palm down above the shoulders. Having folded body, the legs swiftly swing up and forward. Press down with feet, straighten stomach and raise body, causing the back to rise up off the ground, the feet landing under the body, knees bent, the body standing erect. (Diag. A.20.1 and supplementary diag, A.20.2,3)

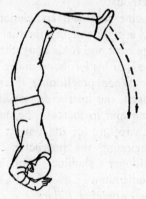

Diag. A. 20.2

Essentials:

The leg thrust, press with feet and straightening of stomach should all be well-timed. If too early or late one will not rise up.

Easily made mistake:

Leg thrust too early or late.

Diag. A. 20.3

Corrective methods:

a) The instructor may aid completion of the movement thus; stand at right side of practitioner. When practitioner pulls legs back and folds body, the instructor may, on one bent knee, put his left hand under the latter's right shoulder blade. When practitioner thrusts the legs and straightens stomach, the instructor may lift upward with left hand, helping him to increase the momentum of the legs and to get a feeling for the timing.

b) At the beginning the instructor can press down above the practitioner's shoulders with both hands, aiding push off momentum.

Black Dragon Entwining Pillar:

a) Left leg bends, then dropping to rest on ground. Right leg is on top of left, slightly bent, the lower parts of both legs spread apart in a scissor shape. Body is supported by the arms on the left side, head turned to right, gaze on right foot. (Diag. A.21.1)

b) The thighs basically do not move, the lower legs crossing outward with force (like scissors crossing). Next,

Diag. A. 21.1   Diag. A. 21.2

straight right leg with hooked foot swings up to upper left of head, left foot follows behind, buttocks and waist leaving ground, back and shoulders leaning back onto ground, hands pressing down in front of shoulders. (Diag. A.21.2)

c) Use the momentum gained by the backward lean of torso and right leg hooking up to swiftly stick out chest and straighten waist, the two feet coming together and kicking up. Push up with hands to body is supported by hands, feet pointing up in a handstand. Then bend waist, folding body so feet come down to ground in front of face, body coming up erect. (Diag. A.21.3)

Essentials:

Swing up of right leg and leaning back of torso must be coordinated as well as swift and strong. When feet are facing upward, the swift sticking out of chest, straightening of waist and pushing down with hands are a continuous movement during which one must not relax nor let them become disjointed.

Easily made mistakes:

a) Legs not performing an upward screwing movement.

b) Untimely sticking out of chest and waist, back not leaving ground, twisting round where they were.

Corrective methods:

a) Become thoroughly proficient in the upward swing of the right leg and the following twisting of the left heel.

b) Practise rolling backward up into a handstand.

Mid-air Side Spin:

Facing East, run forward a couple of steps. When right foot is in front, jump a pace, then leap off swiftly immediately after landing. At same time, left leg is raised, knee bent in front of body. As soon as left foot lands to fore (E), take off with force from ball of foot, the right leg swinging up behind the body. Torso bends forward and, using the leap from the left foot, the two legs soar upward, face looking down, executing a left side roll in mid-air. Right foot lands first, toes facing

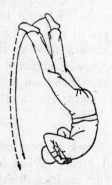

Diag. A. 21.3   Diag. A. 22.1

West, left foot then landing to the rear of the right.
Torso straightens up facing West. (Diags. A.22.1,2,3,4,)

Easily made mistakes:

a) Legs not straight when swung, speed too slow.

b) No force in spring from ground, body tumbling forward.

Corrective methods:

a) First practise a cartwheel to improve swing of legs and grasp the movement.

Diag. A. 22.2

Diag. A. 22.3

Diag. A. 22.4

b) Aid from the instructor, who holds the practitioner by the waist to help the turn, until it can be done without assistance.

c) After the left foot has landed, torso should not fall forward. Emphasize lifting the head and sticking out chest.

Spin:

a) Stand with legs apart. Torso turns to right. Left foot first leaves ground and swings to right. Arms extended level at sides of body. Gaze to right front. (Diag. A.23.1)

b) Left foot steps to the left, and after it lands, ball of the foot grinds to left, leg slightly bent, foot collecting strength in preparation for an upward spring. Body leans forward flat, swinging waist in a spin to back left. At same time, straight arms follow torso in swing to lef rear, right foot following, leaving the ground and swinging upward. Head turns left, body almost level. (Diag. A. 23.2)

c) Carry straight on. Spring off from left foot in a

Diag. A. 23.1

Diag. A. 23.2

leap, body suspended level to form Horizontal Mid-air Spin. Legs spin to left following body, right leg below, left leg swinging up. In mid-air, stick out chest, sink waist, arms swinging upward. Having spun a full revolution, right foot lands first, left after. (Diags. A.23.3,4)

Essentials:

Left foot must spring off with force, so body soars into the air. In mid-air stick chest out and keep head up.

Diag. A. 23.3   Diag. A. 23.4

Legs extended straight, swing up, so body makes a level spin.

Easily made mistakes:

a) During level spin, the mid-air pose may not be precisely balanced, for instance, head dropping, waist bent, legs low or bent.

b) Speed of spin too slow so body cannot make a full revolution.

c) Not enough force in the swing of the waist.

d) After having sprung off, the right leg takes too large a step forward so that the legs cannot swing back.

Corrective methods:

a) Left leg supports body to maintain balanced swallow posture and then spin left as before. (Diag. A.24.1)

b) During level spin, emphasize keeping head up, chest out and legs swinging up.

c) Practise with a support of the hands; starting in the same posture as before, support the body with the hands on something during the left level spin, arms braced, head up, waist sunk, legs swinging so as to appreciate the proper order of the leg's swinging movement.

40

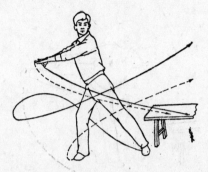

Diag. A. 24.1

Diag. A. 24.2

(Diags. A.24.2,3)

6) Explanation of Terms Used in This Section

Palm:

a) Palm Thrust: Palm facing up or down, straighten arm forward or to upper front, fingers forward.

b) Palm Push: With fingers pointing up and side of little finger facing forward, straighten arm to front or side. So long as palm form does not change, all are palm pushes.

41

Diag. A. 24.3

c) Palm Swing: With palm facing up or down, swing straight arm from down to up, back to front, up to down, front to back or in a circle, all are palm swings.

d) Palm Pull: To take the right palm as example; fingers up, palm facing forward, "Tiger's Mouth" open (thumb splayed), palm swings forward in an arc with bent arm from in front of chest or left side, changing to fist or hook when it reaches limit (or to open palm to grab opponent's hand or arm).

e) Extension: Usually straightening arm from bent to extended or from back to front, all are extensions.

f) Pull Back: Retracting arm to side of body from straight to bent or front to back, all are pull backs.

Arm:

a) Arm bend (elbow bend): Straight arm bending at elbow.

b) Inward turn of forearm: To take right arm as example; extend it straight to front, palm up, thumb pointing right. Forearm revolves left, thumb moving up and left so palm now faces down, thumb pointing left.

c) Outward turn of forearm: To take right arm as example; extend it straight out to front, palm down, thumb pointing left. Forearm revolves right, thumb moving up and right, so palm faces up, thumb pointing right.

Body:

a) Shift weight forward: Stand with feet apart to front and back, body weight starting on back foot, then shifting forward onto front foot.

b) Shift weight backward: Stand with feet apart to front and back, body weight starting on front foot, then shifting back onto back foot.

c) On the waist: On the waist or the sides of the waist means either side of the waist or hips, roughly where one's belt is.

Stances:

a) Front and Back Open Stance: One foot forward, one foot to rear, legs straight or slightly bent at knees.

b) Parallel Open Stance: Feet spread apart parallel to left and right, legs straight or slightly bent at knees.

c) Forward Step: One foot takes a step forward from back to front.

d) Shifting Step: Front foot moving forward a half pace is a Forward Shifting Step. When the back foot takes a half step forward without passing the front foot is a Rear Forward Shifting Step.

e) Traversing Side Step: One foot takes a step crosswise from left to right or right to left.

f) Retreating Step: One foot takes a step backward from in front of body to behind body.

g) Covering Step: One leg supports body, the other

foot turns round other side from front of supporting leg and lands firmly on ground.

h) Penetrating Step: One leg supports the body, the other foot turns round other side from behind supporting leg and lands firmly on ground.

i) Alighting Step: One foot descends to land firmly on ground.

Legs:

a) Bend knees to full squat: Bend legs, upper legs pressed close to lower legs, backside close to heels.

b) Bend knees to half squat: Bend legs, lower legs upright, upper legs level at right angles to them or slightly higher.

c) Legs slightly bent: Knee joints slightly curved.

d) The knee-pit: The hollow part at the back of the knee.

Feet:

a) Toes turned outward: Take toes of the right foot pointing forward (S) as example; using heel as axis, toes swing out from front to right 45° or 90°.

b) Toes pulled (turned) in: Take toes of right foot pointing forward (S) as example; using heel as axis, toes swing in to left 45° or 90°.

c) Ball of foot: The front third of the sole.

d) Full sole: The whole sole of the foot.

e) Stamp: Stamp down with force so the full sole lands flat on the ground making a noise.

Directions:

South — front of chest; North — back; East — left side; West — right side.

Chapter II
THE SINGLE BROADSWORD
AND ITS TECHNIQUES

Section 1
THE BROADSWORD AND ITS PARTS

There are many forms of the broadsword, but here we shall only introduce the form and parts of the single broadsword, as seen in Diag. A.25.

1) Blade: Includes the whole body of the sword except for the hilt and guard.

2) Point: The very tip of the blade. This is usually rounded off for fear of injury during practice or competition.

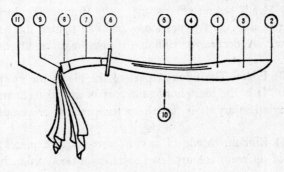

Diag. A. 25

3) Face: The flat surface on either side of the blade. The face is smooth and shiny and touching it should be strictly avoided. In general, the way to admire someone else's sword is to take the hilt in the right hand and rest the blade flat on the sleeve of one's left forearm, so as not to smudge or dampen it and cause rust.

4) Blood ruts: Two channels etched along the face near the back of the blade. Although today of no practical use, they are retained to enhance the beauty of the blade.

5) Back: The thickest part to the blade. Only this part is allowed to stick close to the body and be supported by the hand during various movements.

6) Guard: The round iron guard between the hilt and the blade. Its main use is to protect the hand, especially during practice of duel routines.

7) Hilt: The place gripped by the hand. Made of wood and usually bound with cloth to prevent it from becoming slippery due to perspiration.

8) Head: The tip of the hilt. Prevents the sword from slipping out of one's hand and can also be used for striking the opponent.

9) Head screw: Fixes the hilt firmly. If during practice the guard comes loose, one can tighten the head screw. A decorative ribbon or rings may be attached to it.

10) Edge: The thinnest part of the blade, the cutting edge. It is the most important part in sword technique. To avoid injury, it is not sharp for practice or competition.

11) Ribbon: Made of two or three square pieces of silk of different colours sewn together at one corner then tied through the head screw. The silk should be of thick

material, so the ribbon does not flap about uncontrollably or wrap around the wrist. In the past the ribbon was wrapped around the wrist in battle to prevent the sword slipping from one's grasp, but now it is just for show.

Section 2

GRIPPING TECHNIQUES

If the sword is to be adroitly brandished, one must have a variety of flexibly interchangeable gripping techniques as well as a strong grip. The three main gripping techniques introduced here are used alternately throughout practice with sometimes all three forms being used in the execution of one single sword technique. Therefore, these different gripping techniques must be thoroughly mastered so that they can be flexibly alternated as one wishes. Only then, once the skill has been developed through long practice and their use has become second nature, can one practise the routines properly.

The three main gripping techniques are:

a) Full grip: Fingers and thumb grip hilt firmly, the "Tiger's Mouth" on right palm (Diag. A.26) up close to the guard. Thumb covers and presses down on forefinger (Diag. A.27). For instance, the Parry (Diag. A.28), Concealing (Diag. A.29), Cut (Diag. A.30) and Crosswise Slice (Diag. A.31) all use the full grip.

b) Half grip: Fingers and thumb grip hilt firmly, the second joint on forefinger pressed against the guard and ring finger, little finger and palm-root gripping hilt firmly (Diag. A.32). For instance, the Chop (Diag. A.33), Stab (Diag. A.34), Sweep Thrust (Dig. A.35) and Hack

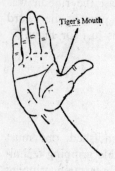

Tiger's Mouth

Diag. A. 26

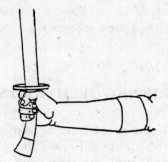

Diag. A. 27

Diag. A. 28

Diag. A. 29

Diag. A. 30

Diag. A. 31

Diag. A. 32

Diag. A. 33

Diag. A 34

Diag. A. 35

Diag. A. 36

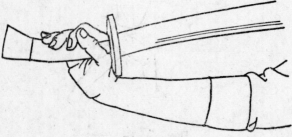

Diag. A. 37

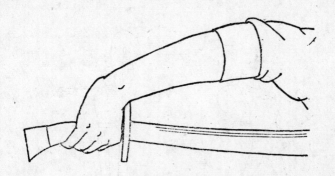

Back View

Diag. A. 38   Diag. A. 39

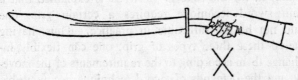

Wrong Gripping Technique

Diag. A. 42

51

Diag. A. 40   Diag. A. 41

(Diag. A.36) all use the half grip.

c) Pincer grip: Grip hilt with fingers and thumb, "Tiger's Mouth" close to guard. Thumb and forefinger grip hilt with force, the other three fingers relax and can sometimes leave hilt (Diag. A.37 and Back View). For instance, the Side Press (Diag. A. 38), Entwining the Head (Diag. A.39), Binding the Head (Diag. A.40) and Back Rest (Diag. A.41) all use the pincer grip.

A mistake often made by beginners is to grip the sword too far from the guard half-way down or at the bottom of the hilt, as in Diag. A.42.

Although for the sake of clarity it is explained that a certain sword technique requires a certain grip, one should not be too inflexible in practice. Thus, having mastered these three types of grip, one can flexibly interchange them according to the requirements of the movement and the demands of sword technique accuracy, becoming thoroughly practised in the sword's basic rules and adapting flexibly according to what feels most effective.

52

Section 3

SWORD TECHNIQUES

1. Concealing
   Level Concealing
   Upright Concealing
   Round the Middle Concealing
2. Entwining the Head
3. Binding the Head
4. Wrist Flourish
   Wrist Shearing Flourish
   Wrist Sweeping Flourish
   Upright Rear Flourish
5. Slice
6. Hack
7. Stab
8. Cut
9. Sweep Thrust
   Straight Sweep Thrust
   Reverse Sweep Thrust
10. Side Press
    Right Side Press
    Left Side Press
11. Chop
    Straight Chop
    Reverse Chop
12. Sweep
13. Wave
14. Swipe
15. Press
16. Vertical Slash
17. Upward Thrust

18. Jab
19. Push
    Vertical Push
    Horizontal Push
20. Back Rest
    Rear Back Rest
    Shoulder Back Rest
21. Parry
22. Side Parry
23. Embracing

1. CONCEALING

1) Level Concealing:

a) Stand upright, feet together, facing South. Right hand holds sword across the front of body, blade-edge down, point facing left. Left arm hangs naturally by side of body. Gaze forward. (Diag. B.1)

b) Feet do not move. Torso turns slightly to left (S-E). Right hand pulls sword to right rear, blade-edge down, point facing lower front. Left arm rises up to side level with shoulder, fingers pointing up, side of little finger pointing ahead to form Upright Palm. Head turns to left, gaze straight ahead along line of left arm. (Diag. B.2)

Essentials:

Legs straight, chest out, stomach in, head up, neck erect. Fingers of left palm as upright as possible, right arm pulled right back.

Easily made mistakes:

a) Right arm not pulled back sufficiently, arm bent too much. (Diag. B.3)

b) When left arm is straight, fingers do not easily face

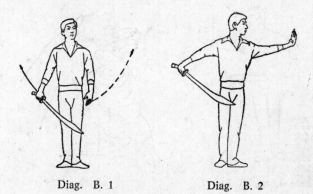

| Diag. B. 1 | Diag. B. 2 |

upward; when they face upward, arm is bent. This is due to insufficient flexibility of wrist joint, so beginners must improve wrist flexibility and gradually reach the required posture.

Practice method:

Right hand grabs hold of left fingers and forcefully presses them leftward, then alternate this with left and right hands. This can be practised any time. (Diag. B.4)

2) Upright Concealing:

Starting posture same as Level Concealing — Diag. B. 2. (Diag. B.5.1)

Feet do not move. Right hand swings sword straight from lower right towards left to left side of waist, wrist straight, palm hollow inward, so the sword rests upright behind left shoulder, point up, blade-edge facing outward. At same time, left arm rises up from left, palm facing up, fingers pointing right. Head turns back to front, gaze forward. (Diag. B.5.2)

Essentials:

Diag. B. 3   Diag. B. 4

Right arm should be extended as far round to left as possible, so sword is vertical at left side. All movements of sword, left arm and head should be completed together.

Easily made mistakes:

a) Right arm bent too much, sticking too close to body.

b) Sword not upright, left arm bent.

Diag. B. 5.1   Diag. B. 5.2

Practice method:

One can practise changing from Level Concealing to Vertical Concealing.

3) Round the Middle Concealing:

Starting posture same as Level Concealing — Diag. B.2. (Diag. B.6.1)

Feet do not move. Right hand swings sword from lower right round to left side of waist, palm facing down, so sword is horizontal and close to left side of waist, point to rear, blade-edge facing outward. Left arm rises up from left, palm up, fingers pointing right. Head turns left, gaze forward. (Diag. B.6.2)

Diag. B. 6.1   Diag. B. 6.2

Essentials:

Right arm slightly bent to maintain a curve. Keep sword level, the middle of the sword-back sticking closely to the left side of body. The sword swing, rise of left arm and turning of head should all be completed together.

Easily made mistakes:

a) Right arm bent too much, the inside of it too close to body.

b) Sword not level.

Practice method:

Practise the change from Level Concealing to Round the Middle Concealing.

2. ENTWINING THE HEAD

Starting posture same as Level Concealing — Diag. B.2. (Diag. B.7.1)

a) Feet do not move. Torso turns slightly to right (S). Right hand raises sword with straight arm, so sword, point downward, moves left across body and round left shoulder, sword back facing inward, point down and blade-edge out. Left arm bends at elbow, bringing left palm in front of right chest, fingers pointing up, palm facing right. Gaze to front. (Diag. B.7.2)

b) Continue straight on. Right hand swings sword round rear, sticking close to back, moving on round to right past right shoulder to the right side of body, arm straight at shoulder height, palm of gripping hand facing up, point right, blade-edge forward. Left arm swings out

Diag. B. 7.1   Diag. B 7.2

level to left from in front of chest, until it is extended straight to left side at shoulder height, palm forward, fingers pointing left. Head turns right, gaze on sword point. (Diag. B.7.3)

Essentials:

As right hand passes around back, right arm should be raised as high as possible, sword sticking close to shoulders all the way around the back, and with sword always pointing down. The movement of left arm from straight to bent, bent to straight must be coordinated with movement of sword. Entwining the Head uses the Pincer Grip, thumb and forefinger tight, the other three fingers relaxed.

Easily made mistakes:

a) Right arm bent too much while Entwining, the Head, gripping hand too close to top of head. (Diag. B.8)

b) Sword only swinging level round top of head, not passing shoulders and back. (Diag. B.9)

c) Lowering head and bending waist while blade circles round.

Diag. B. 7.3

Diag. B. 8

Practice method:
Practise strictly according to the prescribed technique, starting slowly, then gradually speeding up movement.

3. BINDING THE HEAD

Start from the finishing posture of Entwining the Head — Diag. B.7.3. (Diag. B.10.1 and Rear View)

a) Feet do not move. Right arm raises sword to rear from right side so sword points down, circling round back from right to left to behind left shoulder, blade-edge facing rear. At same time, left arm bends at elbow, palm brought in in front of right chest, fingers up, palm facing right. Head turns back left to front, gaze forward. (Diag. B.10.2 and Rear View)

b) Continue straight on. Right hand continues to circle round left shoulder past front of body and down to lower right, pulling back sword to form Level Concealing. Left arm extends straight out to left at shoulder height, fingers up, palm edge left. Gaze on left palm. (Diag. B.10.3 and Rear View)

Diag. B. 9   Diag. B. 10.1

Diag. B. 10.2   Diag. B. 10.3

Essentials:

Binding the Head follows the same route as Entwining the Head in reverse. The hand holding the sword should be raised as high as possible, the sword sticking close to the shoulders and back as it circles round, keeping it vertical, point down. Swing of left arm must also be well coordinated.

Easily made mistakes:

a) Right arm bent, sword too far away from body as it circles shoulders and back, so that it swings round horizontally by the top of the head.

b) Dropping head or bending waist.

Practice method:

Same as for Entwining the Head.

4. WRIST FLOURISH

For the movements and diagrams of the Wrist Shearing Flourish, Wrist Sweeping Flourish and the Upright Rear

Flourish, see the single broadsword basic movements second set in the the fourth section of Chapter II.

5. SLICE

Starting posture same as Level Concealing — Diag. B.2. (Diag. B.11.1)

a) Feet do not move. Torso turns slightly to right (S-W). Right forearm twists outward, following the turn of body it rises up level to right side, blade-edge down, point right, sword and arm forming a straight line. Left arm bends at elbow, left palm coming in to in front of right chest, palm down, fingers pointing to right shoulder. Head turns right, gaze on sword point. (Diag. B.11.2)

Diag. B. 11.1   Diag. B. 11.2

b) Torso turns left (S-E). At same time, forearm of right hand twists outward, rising up with a straight arm so blade-edge faces forward, point slanting back and up. Left arm does not move. Head turns left, gaze forward. (Diag. B.11.3)

c) Left foot takes a step forward (E), left knee bend-

Diag. B. 11.3

ing to half squat, right leg extended to form Left Bow
Stance. At same time, right hand slashes forward from
above with straight arm, so blade-edge faces down, point
forward (E), sword and arm forming a straight line. Left
palm swings from right shoulder down, left and to rear
in an arc to the left side of body level with shoulder, palm
facing outward. Gaze on sword point. (Diag. B.11.4)

Essentials:

Diag. B. 11.4

Diag. B. 12   Diag. B. 13.1

The three movements must be completed successively. Left Bow Stance, Slice and Left Palm Swing to rear should be completed together. The swing of the sword up and forward from rear should form a curve. When slicing, wrist should use strength so force penetrates through to blade-edge.

Easily made mistakes:

Route of Slice not a curve, wrist no force, so centre of force does not reach blade-edge.

Practice method:

Stand erect, raise sword with right arm straight obliquely upward, bending wrist backward so the blade-edge faces upward. Next move arm forward, adding momentum with wrist and hand, so sword slices down forward. Then raise it back up and repeat the movement again and again. (Diag. B.12)

6. HACK

Starting posture is the same as Level Concealing — Diag. B.2. (Diag. B.13.1)

a) Feet do not move. Torso turns to right. Right forearm twists outward, following the turn of the torso to swing up extended level on right side, blade-edge forward, point right. At same time, left arm bends at elbow, left palm brought in in front of right chest, palm down, fingers right. Head turns right, gaze on sword point. (Diag. B.13.2)

Diag. B. 13.2

b) Torso turns left, left foot taking a pace forward (E), knee bending to half squat, right leg extended to form Left Bow Stance. At same time, right hand swings sword from right side to lower left in a Hack. Left palm rests on right forearm. Gaze downward along hacking sword. (Diag. B.13.3)

Essentials:

Turning right of torso, twisting outward and raising level of right forearm and bending of left arm should all be completed together. Left Bow Stance, Hack, and movement of left hand down onto right forearm should all be completed together. When hacking, the arm should be relaxed, and as it approaches finish wrist should add

Diag. B. 13.3

momentum. This sudden burst of force will enable the centre of force to reach the blade-edge. Sword and arm must form a straight line.

Easily made mistakes:

Arm and sword not in line during Hack, resulting in no speed or strength and the centre of force not reaching the blade-edge.

Practice method:

Stand with legs apart to left and right, left hand on waist, right arm holding sword rising obliquely to upper right, then hacking from upper right obliquely down to lower left. Continue straight on raising sword to upper left, hacking from upper left obliquely down to lower right, and so on, repeating this to left and right again and again. Long practice of this will increase hacking speed, force reaching down to the blade-edge. (Diags. B.14.1,2, 3,4)

7. STAB

Starting posture same as Level Concealing — Diag. B.2.

Diag. B. 14.1   Diag. B. 14.2

(Diag. B.15.1)

Level Stab:

Left foot takes a step forward (E), bending at knee to half squat, right leg straightening to form Left Bow Stance. At same time, right arm extends sword straight forward in Level Stab, point forward, blade-edge down. Fingers of left palm rest on inside of right forearm. Gaze on sword point. (Diag. B.15.2)

Diag. B. 14.3   Diag. B. 14.4

Diag. B. 15.1

Diag. B. 15.2

Essentials:

Stab, Left Bow Stance and left palm resting on right inner forearm should all be completed together. Force must reach sword point, sword at same height as shoulders, sword and arm in a straight line. Stabbing arm must go from bent to straight.

Easily made mistakes:

Stabbing forward with arm already straight, as a result of which strength does not reach sword point.

Practice method:

Practise raising sword to Stab, emphasizing the arm going from bent to straight.

8. CUT

Starting posture same as Level Concealing — Diag. B.2. (Diag. B.16.1)

a) Left foot takes a step backward (W), right knee bending, left leg straightening, torso turning somewhat to right. Right hand holding sword does not move. Left palm moves from left side front down to right to rest on right forearm. Head turns right, gaze on sword body. (Diag. B.16.2)

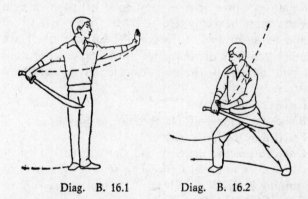

Diag. B. 16.1   Diag. B. 16.2

b) Left foot crosses behind right, ball of foot touching ground, legs squatting down fully to Rest Stance. At same time, right hand swings sword obliquely to lower right in a Cut, blade-edge slanting down, point forward (S). Left palm extends up from forearm to above head, palm slanting to upper left, fingers pointing left. Head

69

Diag. B. 16.3

dropped down slightly, gaze on sword body. (Diag. B.16.3)

Essentials:

Right foot's pace back and resting of left palm on right forearm must be completed together. Arm and sword should be at an angle of about 65° during Cut. Force should reach front of blade-edge. Rest Stance, downward cut and raising of left palm should all be completed together.

Easily made mistakes:

Blade-edge ending up facing down or forwards.

Practice method:

One can practise the Stab and Cut together. First do Level Stab from Level Concealing stance, then carry on by turning body to right rear. Left foot crosses behind right to form Rest Stance, right arm cutting downward. Having done that, rise up and turn body, stepping out to front to form Left Bow Stance and Level Stab. Repeat this again and again.

There is also a High Stab, where the sword is above shoulder height (Diag. B.17) and a Low Stab, where it is level with knee (Diag. B.18).

Diag. B. 17

Diag. B. 18

9. SWEEP THRUST

Starting posture same as Level Concealing — Diag. B.2. (Diag. B.19.1)

Straight Sweep Thrust:

Toes of left foot turn outward, right foot then taking a step forward(E), knee bending to half squat, left foot straightening to form Right Bow Stance. At same time, right forearm twists outward, so blade-edge faces forward, sword swinging forward in

71

Diag. B. 19.1

Diag. B. 19.2

a Sweep Thrust at knee height, blade-edge up, point forward, gripping hand palm up. Left palm swings from original position up and back with body so it is extended at shoulder height at left side, palm forward. Gaze on sword point. (Diag. B.19.2)

Reverse Sweep Thrust:

Continuing from above posture, left heel rises, pivoting on ball of foot as heel turns outward, the torso thus turning right. Right foot follows turn of body and is collected in in front of left foot, toes touching ground. At same time, right forearm turns inward and is brought in in front of body along with right foot, blade-edge facing right, point down. Fingers of left palm rest on back of right palm. Head turns right, gaze forward. (Diag. B.20.1)

Diag. B. 20.1

Carry straight on. Torso turns a bit further to right. Right foot takes a step forward(W), knee bending to half squat, left leg straightening to form Right Bow Stance. At same time, right hand swings sword to right side following step out of right foot in a Reverse Sweep Thrust, blade-edge up, point forward. Left hand leaves back of right hand and rises level on left side of body, palm forward. Gaze on sword point. (Diag. B.20.2)

Essentials:

Right Bow Stance and Straight Sweep Thrust should be completed together. Force must reach blade-edge. Turn of body to Right Bow Stance and Reverse Sweep Thrust should be completed together. The extension of

Diag. B. 20.2

arm during Sweep Thrust should follow shoulder.

Easily made mistakes:

a) Right arm not straight during Sweep Thrust, so it cannot follow shoulder and stretch out far.

b) Stance and Sweep Thrust not completed together.

Practice method:

Straight and Reverse Sweep Thrusts can be practised repeatedly from side to side, and can be practised changing from Right Bow Stance to Left Bow Stance, at the same time becoming accustomed to the movement and

Diag. B. 21.1

74

Diag. B. 21.2

use of force in the Sweep Thrust. (Diag. B.21.1,2) The Straight or Reverse Sweep Thrust can also be practised by swinging the sword right round in a circle.

10. SIDE PRESS

Starting posture same as Level Concealing — Diag. B.2. (Diag. B.22.1)

Left Side Press:

Left foot takes half pace forward (E), toes touching ground to form Point Stance. At same time, right hand swings sword backward, the forearm twisting outward and when arm has swung so sword and arm form a straight line level with shoulder, wrist bends upward so sword point faces upward, sword body at 90° to right arm. At this point keep straight arm swinging upward without stopping, until sword is horizontal above top of head, blade-edge facing up, point left. Left arm does not move. Gaze forward past left palm. (Diag. B.22.2)

Continue straight on. Left foot takes another half step forward(E), toes turning outward, knee bending forward.

Diag. B. 22.1   Diag. B. 22.2

Right leg is straight, heel rising off floor. At same time, arm and sword still maintain 90° angle, and continue from above, forward and to lower left in an arcing Side Press, blade-edge down, point to rear. Left palm presses on right wrist during downward Side Press. Gaze on sword point. (Diag. B.22.3)

Right Side Press:

From above posture. Right foot steps forward(E), toes turning out as they touch ground, knee bending forward. Left leg straightens, heel rises off floor. At same time, right arm bends a moment, bringing sword from lower left in an arc up and forward to lower right, then up again in a Side Press, blade-edge now facing right, point up. When the sword reaches lower right, left palm leaves right wrist and is raised up past head, palm up, fingers pointing right. Gaze on sword point. (Diag. B. 22.4)

Essentials:

Left and Right Side Presses must be coordinated with left and right steps. During Side Press, sword and arm must maintain 90°. Arm must be straight, sword keeping

76

| Diag. B. 22.3 | Diag. B. 22.4 |

close to side of body, sword moving on a circular path. The Side Press is usually done with a pincer grip, thumb and forefinger gripping tightly, point of force reaching sword back. Head and gaze should turn in accordance with movement of Side Press, gaze on sword route.

Easily made mistakes:

a) Side Press and step not coordinated, sometimes stepping first then pressing, at others pressing first then stepping.

b) Sword and arm not at 90° angle. Arm not straight.

c) Point of force not reaching back of sword.

d) Route of Side Press not circular, sword too far from body.

Practice method:

Stand upright without moving feet, only doing the Side Press to left and right, waist turning to follow movement of sword. One can also practise the full Side Press repeatedly advancing forward.

11. CHOP

Starting posture same as Level Concealing — Diag. B.2.

Diag. B. 23.1

(Diag. B.23.1)

Straight Chop:

A Straight Chop is performing a Level Chop from right to left with palm of gripping hand up.

Left foot takes a step forward(E), knee bends to half squat, right leg straightens to form Left Bow Stance. At same time, right forearm twists outward, right hand moving to right rear raised level with shoulder, sword and arm forming a straight line. Sword swings round to front of body, blade-edge forward, in a Level Chop, blade-edge now facing left, point forward, palm of gripping hand up. Left arm swings from front left back to left rear, arm slightly bent, palm down, fingers forward. Gaze on sword point. (Diag. B.23.2)

Reverse Chop:

A Reverse Chop is performing a Level Chop from left to right with palm down.

From above posture, torso turns to right rear (chest facing South). Right leg bends (facing West), left leg

Diag. B. 23.2

straightens to form Right Bow Stance. At same time, right forearm twists inward so blade-edge faces right and, following turn of torso, it makes a level swing to right in a Reverse Chop, gripping palm down, blade-edge to rear, point right. Left arm extends out from left side of body, palm down, fingers pointing left. Gaze on blade-edge. (Diag. B.23.3)

Essentials:

During the level swing of the Chop, there should be a slight angle between sword and arm, so when Chop

Diag. B. 23.3

79

reaches finish, the wrist snaps straight, directing the force on to the blade-edge. The Chop should be at shoulder height.

Easily made mistakes:

a) Sword and arm in a straight line during Chop, so it lacks speed or strength, point of force unclear.

b) Route of Chop uneven, wavering up and down.

Practice method:

One can repeatedly practise the Straight and Reverse Chops together, concentrating on increasing the snapping power of the wrist.

12. SWEEP

Starting posture same as Level Concealing — Diag. B.2. (Diag. B.24.1)

Diag. B. 24.1

Left foot takes a step forward(E), knee bending to half squat, right leg straightening to form Left Side Bow Stance. At same time, right forearm twists outward, right hand swinging sword level to rear, and when sword and arm form a straight line with blade-edge forward(S), torso bends forward and sword sweeps round in an arc to front and left, parallel and close to ground with arm kept straight. Left hand rises from left front to upper left, palm facing left, fingers up. Gaze on sword body. (Diag. B.24.2)

Diag. B. 24.2

Continue straight on. Pivoting on ball of left foot, turn 180° to left rear(W), right foot pulled back to beside left foot (toes of both feet pointing West). As body turns, knees gradually bend down to full squat. At same time, right arm, straight and stretched out to full, continues level sweep round in an arc close to ground, until it points forward, blade-edge facing left. Left hand stays above head, palm up, fingers pointing right. Gaze on sword body. (Diag. B.24.3)

Essentials:

When squating one must maintain an erect waist, chest expanded. The spin should be fast and powerful. The Sweep of the sword should be round. For a whole Sweep or more the sword should remain level with ground, about 10 cm. or so from the ground. During Sweep arm should

Diag. B. 24.3

be completely extended.

Easily made mistakes:

a) Bending the back and waist when squatting down, lowering the head.

b) The Sweep uneven, sometimes high, sometimes low. Turn of body disjointed, speed uneven.

c) Arm too bent during Sweep.

Practice method:

Just practise half-squatting down and spinning round in the Leg Sweep without the sword. Gradually increase to full squat for a full turn or even more. Add the sword once one has mastered the Leg Sweep.

13. WAVE

Starting posture same as Level Concealing — Diag. B. 2. (Diag. B.25.1)

Take a half step forward(E) with left foot, knee slightly bent, right leg straight. At same time, swing sword from lower right front to front of body, sword and arm forming a straight line, blade-edge right, point forward and down. Left hand moves down to rest as support on right forearm, palm down. Gaze forward. (Diag. B.25.2)

Diag. B. 25.1   Diag. B. 25.2

Continue straight on. Torso leans back, head raised. Right arm bends slightly, wrist twisting strongly to left, so with sword-back facing body, sword swings from lower front to left and up, blade-edge facing left, point upward. Left hand remains on right lower forearm. (Diag. B.25.3)

Continue straight on. Feet do not move. Wrist continues twist round (now to right), so sword waves in a slanting circle from upper position to right and down to lower front. Left hand still rests on lower right forearm. (Diag. B.25.4)

Essentials:

The movement of sword should be due solely to the twist of the right wrist. The Wave should be circular, both fast and powerful. The sword should stick close to body during Wave, and as it moves close one must coordinate the backward inclination of torso.

Easily made mistakes:

83

Diag. B. 25.3   Diag. B. 25.4

Wave too slow, not circular and too far from body, wrist unable to exert strength, arm too bent.

Practice method:

The Wave should be done with the pincer grip and one should practise vertical and horizontal brandishes, so that the Wave has speed and strength. Wave above the head can be done with bent or straight arm. (Diag. B. 26)

Diag. B. 26   Diag. B. 27

There is also the Side Wave, and when doing this one must lean to the left. (Diag. B.27)

14. SWIPE

Starting posture same as Level Concealing — Diag.B.2. (Diag. B.28.1)

Diag. B. 28.1

Feet do not move. Right forearm turns outward, arm extended straight, jabbing straight to front, blade-edge facing left, point forward, sword and arm at shoulder

Diag. B. 28.2

height. Left hand rests on right wrist. Gaze on blade-edge. (Diag B.28.2)

Left Swipe:

From above position. Left foot takes a step backward(W), leg slightly bent, body weight shifting to left leg. Torso turns slightly to left. At same time, right hand swings sword level in an arc to left, so blade-edge swipes level to left, point of force reaching centre of blade-edge. Left hand still rests on right wrist. Gaze on blade-edge. (Diag. B.28.3)

Right Swipe:

From above posture, right foot takes a pace backward (W), leg slightly bent, weight shifting to right leg. Torso turns slightly to right. At same time, right forearm turns inward, right palm facing down, blade-edge facing right, blade making a Level Swipe in a curve from left side to front then to right side, point of force reaching centre of blade-edge. Left palm still rests on right wrist. Gaze on blade-edge. (Diag. B.28.4)

Essentials:

Diag. 28.3   Diag. B. 28.4

Swipe and retreating step should be coordinated. Right arm is slightly bent during Swipe, sword body level, blade-edge outward, point of force reaching centre of blade-edge, with an outward pushing force and outward curving form. Forearm turns inward in change from left swipe to right swipe, though there should be no change up or down in sword body's position, the sword position remaining the same, the sword merely revolving.

Easily made mistakes:

a) Right arm too bent during Swipe, sword not swinging in an arc but forming a Pull instead.

b) The wrist twisting down as it turns in the change from Left to Right Swipe, causing the blade-point to rise up or swing to left.

Practice method:

Grasp correctly the movements for both types of Swipe, then repeatedly practise them to left and right. There is also a Level Swipe with full turn, and when swiping, the arm is extended straight, blade-edge facing out, pushing outward in an arc.

15. PRESS

Starting posture same as Level Concealing — Diag. B.2. (Diag.B.29.1)

Right foot takes a step to rear(W), toes turning outward, knee bending to full squat, left leg extended straight, toes pulled to form Left Crouching Stance. At same time, left hand moves down to press down on right wrist, the aiding force making the sword press downward, blade-edge down, point facing East, sword level with left leg, blade-edge close to ground. Gaze forward. (Diag. B.29.2)

Diag. B. 29.1   Diag. B. 29.2

Essentials:

Crouching Stance and Press should be completed together. When going down to meet the sword, arms should be straight, left hand pressing on right wrist to give extra force. Blade-edge must not touch ground.

Easily made mistakes:

a) Crouching Stance and Press not coordinated.

b) Press too weak, sword not level, hilt and sword body too close to leg.

c) Right arm bent, sword too far from ground.

Practice method:

From standing erect in Concealing Stance, go down to Crouching Stance with Press. When this is completed, rise up with left leg bent forward, right leg extended straight to form a Bow Step with Stab, then bring up right leg together with left to form Erect Concealing Stance. Repeat again and again. The Press is also done with the left hand pressing on the front of the sword-back. (Diag. B.30)

16. VERTICAL SLASH

Starting posture same as Level Concealing — Diag. B.2. (Diag. B.31.1)

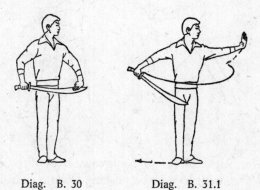

Diag. B. 30   Diag. B. 31.1

Left leg takes a half step backward(W) to form an Open Stance. At same time, right forearm turns inward so sword points down, arm straight out to front, right palm facing outward, blade-edge left. Left hand rests on right wrist. Next, torso turns left, right arm swinging in a Vertical Slash to left side. Gaze on blade-edge. (Diag. B.31.2)

Right leg takes a step backward(W), leg slightly bent, left leg straightening, torso turning to right. At same time, wrist bends forward with force, arm bending slightly so blade-edge faces right. Then following turn of torso to right, perform a right Vertical Slash. Left hand still on right wrist. Gaze on blade-edge. (Diag. B.31.3)

Essentials:

Retreating Step and Vertical Slash must be completed together. The point of force must reach blade-edge, so the wrist must be turned outward for Left Slash, then in-

Diag. B. 31.2   Diag. B. 31.3

ward for Right Slash, so blade-edge faces direction of turn. The strength must be pushing towards outside.

Easily made mistakes:

a) Gripping hand raised too high.

b) Sword not straight and too near to body.

Practice method:

Practise the Slash to left and right, then return to Level Concealing. There is also a revolving Vertical Slash, requiring a whole revolution and more. When turning the body, right knee is raised, left leg straight and then, pivoting on ball of foot, turn to rear. Right arm must remain extended, left hand placed on right forearm. (Diag. B.32)

17. UPWARD THRUST

Starting posture same as Level Concealing — Diag. B.2. (Diag. B.33.1)

Feet do not move. Right hand stabs sword forward(E) with straight arm, sword and arm in a straight line at

| Diag. B. 32 | Diag. B. 33.1 |

shoulder height. Left hand rests on right wrist. Gaze on sword-point. (Diag. B.33.2)

Carry straight on. Sink right wrist so hand turns upward, flicking up the point of the sword, focus of force reaching sword-point. Left hand still rests on right wrist. Gaze on sword-point. (Diag. B.33.3)

Essentials:

The Upward Thrust requires fierce sinking of the wrist, the sword-point flicking upward with speed and power,

| Diag. B. 33.2 | Diag. B. 33.3 |

focus of force reaching sword-point. Right arm should remain straight, wrist, forearm and elbow bent downward, sword-point not above head.

Easily made mistakes:

a) Right arm bending too much.

b) Sinking without force, not suddenly bending wrist and arm.

18. JAB

Continuing from the above Upward Thrust. Arm suddenly snaps straight, raising wrist, right palm facing down so sword-point jabs down from above, focus of force reaching point. Left hand still rests on right wrist. Gaze on sword-point. (Diag. B.33.4)

Essentials:

The Jab also requires fiercely straightening the arm and raising the wrist, only in this way will the point have force in the downward jab. The wrist should rise to just above height of shoulder.

Easily made mistakes:

Hunching the shoulders and raising the elbow, and lifting wrist too high so the jab has no force.

Practice method:

Practise Upward Thrust and Jab repeatedly in combination. Just practise with single arm, not resting left hand on wrist, left hand raised up above head. (Diag. B.34.1,2)

19. PUSH

Starting posture same as Level Concealing — Diag. B.2. (Diag. B.35.1)

Diag. B. 33.4   Diag. B. 34.1

Diag. B. 34.2   Diag. B. 35.1

Vertical Push:

Feet do not move. Forearm of right hand twists inward, arm bending so sword is raised in front of chest, point facing down, blade-edge forward, forearm level with shoulder. Left hand rests on lower part of sword-back, palm facing out, fingers pointing left. Gaze forward. (Diag. B.35.2)

Continue straight on. Arms straighten forward

abruptly in a Push. Gaze on sword-body. (Diag. B.35.3)

Essentials:

Arms should push out together with force. Blade-edge must point forward, torso tilting forward slightly to add extra force to the Push.

Easily made mistakes:

Sword not erect. Push lacking force.

Horizontal Push:

From previous posture. Bend both arms and pull sword up in front of chest. Then turn arms so sword is horizontal across chest, point facing left, blade-edge forward. Gaze forward. (Diag. B.35.4)

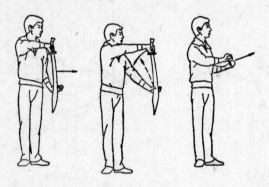

Diag. B. 35.2   Diag. B. 35.3   Diag. B. 35.4

Straighten arms abruptly out forward, sword level with shoulders to form Horizontal Push. Gaze on sword-body. (Diag. B.35.5)

Essentials:

Arms must exert force simultaneously when executing Push, the sword remaining level and firm.

Easily made mistakes:

Sword not level. Push no force.

Diag. B. 35.5

Diag. B. 36.1

Practice method:

One can alternately practise the Vertical and Horizontal Pushes, finishing in the Level Concealing posture. There is also a Backward Push; bend the legs to kneel down on one knee, the other leg bent out in front. When executing Push, torso leans back, head raised. As with the Horizontal Push, first bring arms in in front of chest then past face up and back until arms are extended behind head. (Diag. B.36.1,2)

Diag. B. 36.2

20. BACK REST

Starting posture same as Level Concealing — Diag. B.2. (Diag. B. 37.1)

Rear Back Rest:

Feet do not move. Arm extends straight out from below with blade-edge down, arm and sword forming a straight line, rising with a straight arm forward, then up and back until the sword-back is close to right shoulder blade, sword-point down, blade-edge to rear. As right arm stretches forward, left hand rests on right wrist and follows the right hand up, arm bending slightly, palm facing forward. (Diag. B.37.2, Side View)

Diag. B. 37.1   Diag. B. 37.2

Essentials:

Right arm must be straight. Employ pincer grip. Sword-back should be close to right shoulder.

Easily made mistakes:

Right arm not straight.

Shoulder Rest:

Feet do not move. Right arm extends straight out to

side at shoulder height, and when sword and arm have formed a straight line, bend hand upward so sword moves from right, up, then to left, sword-back touching right shoulder, sword point facing left, blade-edge facing up. Left hand moves from front to up above head, palm up, fingers pointing right. Head turns to right, gaze forward. (Diag. B.37.3)

Essentials:

Use force with the wrist when flicking sword up, arm remaining straight.

Easily made mistakes:

Inability to straighten arm, flicking of sword no force.

Practice method:

Exercise wrist strength by repeating the flick up with straight arm, so sword has speed and strength, and so one can accurately and smoothly place sword along right arm.

21. PARRY

Starting posture same as Level Concealing — Diag. B.2. (Diag. B.38.1)

Feet do not move.   Right forearm turns inward, so

Diag. B. 37.3   Diag. B. 38.1

sword is horizontal in front of stomach, point facing left, blade-edge down. Then raise wrist and straighten arm up past face to above head in a Parry. At same time left forearm turns inward, palm facing down. Bend arm outside sword from in front of chest, straightening arm down to form downward Palm Press, fingers pointing right. Raise head and look at sword-body. (Diag. B.38.2)

Essentials:

Upward Parry and Downward Press should be completed together. The parrying arm must be straight, focus of force reaching blade-edge, the Parry going from bent arm in front of and close to torso to straight up above.

Easily made mistakes:

a) Parry not higher than head.

b) Sword not level, Parry no force.

c) Sword too far from body during upward motion.

Practice method:

Repeatedly practise the raising of wrist and Upward Parry. When coming down, turn the wrist down so the blade-edge faces down in a Press.

There is also the technique of bending the arm and turning the palm of the gripping hand inward so blade-edge faces up, point faces right, in a horizontal Parry across chest. Next straighten arm up above head for Upward Parry. (Diag. 39.1,2)

22. SIDE PARRY

Starting posture same as Level Concealing — Diag. B.2. (Diag. B.40.1)

Feet do not move. Right arm stabs forward with straight arm, blade-edge down, point forward. Left hand rests on right wrist. Gaze at sword-point. (Diag. B.40.2)

Diag. B. 38.2   Diag. B. 39.1   Diag. B. 39.2

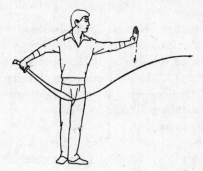

Diag. B. 40.1

Torso turns slightly to right. Right foot takes a Reverse Step backward(W), knee bending to half squat, left leg straightening to form Right Side Bow Stance. At same time, right forearm turns inward, right palm turning outward, so blade-edge points up. Then bend right arm and pull it up from left to right side, right hand higher than shoulder, the sword-point slightly lower; left hand still rests on right wrist. Head turns left, gaze forward.

99

Diag. B. 40.2

(Diag. B.40.3)

Essentials:

The right turn, Reverse Step becoming Side Bow Stance and the inward turn and pull of right arm should all be completed together. Side Parry should be forceful, focus of force reaching the blade-edge. Having completed the Side Parry, one should bend right arm and drop elbow, torso leaning slightly to right.

Easily made mistakes:

a) Side Bow Stance and Side Parry not coordinated.

b) Parry no force, focus of force unclear.

c) Hunching shoulders or raising elbows after completion.

Practice method:

Having finished the Side Parry, bring feet together in a Forward Stab. Repeat this again and again, finally finishing in Level Concealing.

23. EMBRACING

Vertical Embracing:

Feet do not move. Embrace sword in left hand, the

holding method for the five fingers being: thumb on top of the guard (to one side of the sword-blade), forefinger down front of sword-hilt, the other three fingers round the back of the handle, all five fingers gripping tightly around guard so the sword-back nestles close in to the forearm, sword-point upward, blade-edge outward. Arms hang down by sides, shoulders pulled back slightly. Gaze forward. (Diag. B.41).

Horizontal Embracing:

Feet do not move. Left hand embraces sword in same way as above, arms raised and extended straight out forward, blade-edge pointing up, point facing backward. Right hand rests on left forearm. Gaze forward. (Diag. B.42)

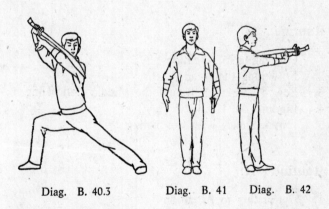

Diag. B. 40.3   Diag. B. 41   Diag. B. 42

Essentials:

Sword must nestle close to left forearm, wrist pulled up and in slightly. Stick out chest, waist erect, both arms slightly bent.

Easily made mistakes:

Arms too bent, so sword does not nestle closely in to

left arm.

Practice Method:

Embracing with the left hand is an important movement in sword routines, it being used at the start and
finish of each routine. Especially during competition,
since it signals the start and finish, it may be held for
some time. Thus it has an important effect on whether
one's sword skills are well perfected or not.

Section 4

TITLES OF BASIC SINGLE
BROADSWORD MOVEMENTS

Routine I:

1. Concealing to Attention
2. Entwining the Head
3. Bow Stance with Round the Middle Concealing
4. Binding the Head
5. Empty Stance with Concealing

Routine II:

1. Concealing to Attention
2. Left Bow Stance with Stab
3. Turn with Right Bow Stance and Slice
4. Left and Right Wrist Shearing Flourish
5. Turn with Right Bow Stance and Sweep Thrust
6. Wrist Sweeping Flourish
7. Turn with Right Bow Stance and Slice

8. Vertical Back Flourish

Routine I:

1. CONCEALING TO ATTENTION

Stand to attention facing South. Torso turns slightly to left. Right hand pulls sword to right rear with straight arm to form Concealing posture. Left arm extends straight out forward in a Palm Push, fingers up, side of little finger forward. Head turns left, gaze in direction of left hand. (Diag. C.1)

2. ENTWINING THE HEAD

a) Feet and torso do not move. With straight arm, right hand swings sword past right side up in a curve to outside front of body, point down, blade-edge facing out, then round left shoulder. Left arm bends at elbow, left hand pulled in in front of chest, fingers pointing up, palm outward. Gaze forward. (Diag. C.2.1)

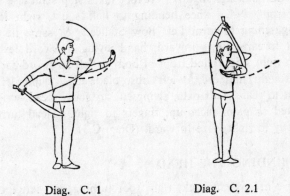

Diag. C. 1   Diag. C. 2.1

b) Carry straight on. Right hand continues rightward swing round the back. When past right shoulder, arm extends out, sword and arm forming a straight line, blade-edge forward, point facing right. Left palm swings out in curve from in front of chest to left side, palm pointing down. Head turns left, gaze on left palm. (Diag. C.2.2)

Diag. C. 2.2

3. BOW STANCE WITH ROUND THE MIDDLE CONCEALING

Bend both legs slightly, left foot takes step slantwise to left front (N-E), knee bending to half squat, right leg straightening to form Left Bow Stance. At same time, right forearm turns inward, hand swinging sword level from right side, round front of body to left so sword-back is brought in close to left ribs, blade-edge facing left, point to rear. Left palm swings up to above head, wrist slanted so palm faces up, fingers to right. Head turns slightly to right, gaze forward. (Diag. C.3)

4. BINDING THE HEAD

a) Shift weight back, right foot turning out, left foot

Diag. C. 3

turning in, torso turning round to right rear. Right leg
bends slightly, left leg straightens to form Right Side Bow
Stance. At same time, right hand swings sword horizontally forward and round to right. Left palm moves
straight out to left side, palm down. Head follows
rightward turn of sword, gaze on sword-body. (Diag.
C.4.1)

b) Carry straight on. Torso turns slightly to left.
Right foot turns in, left foot is pulled up, toes touching

Diag. C. 4.1

ground by right instep, both legs bending to form T-Stance. At same time, right hand rises up, so point is down, blade-edge facing rear, passing round right shoulder to behind back. Left hand bends at elbow, left palm brought in in front of chest, palm facing out, fingers up. Head turns left, gaze forward. (Diag. C.4.2)

5. EMPTY STANCE WITH CONCEALING

Torso turns slightly left. Left foot shifts forward (E), knee bends slightly, toes touching ground. Right leg bends to half squat to form Left Empty Stance. At same time, right hand comes back round left shoulder past front to right rear to form Concealing posture. Left hand extends out to form Upright Palm, fingers up, side of little finger forward. Gaze in direction of left palm. (Diag. C.5)

Diag. C. 4.2   Diag. C. 5

Essentials:

a) Concealing to Attention requires both legs to be straight, chest out, stomach in. The point of the sword should be close to right thigh.

b) Entwining the Head must be smoothly executed, the swing of the two arms well coordinated.

c) The left leg step and swing of two arms during the Round the Middle Concealing must be completed together. Right shoulder should be pulled in, arm curving outward. Left shoulder should be pulled back, arm straight.

d) Binding the Head must be executed smoothly, swing of two arms well coordinated.

e) The shift forward of left foot, the Concealing and the Palm Push in Empty Stance with Concealing should all be completed together.

The above movements are really a complete Entwining the Head and Binding the Head. This combination is one of the most common of the basic sword movements and so they should be practised repeatedly, gradually increasing the speed until they can be done perfectly and comfortably. What is the difference between them? In general, when the blade-edge faces out, sword point down, moving from in front of head to left, round left shoulder past back to right is called Entwining the Head. When the sword moves from the right side back round the back to the left, round the left shoulder and to front, this is called Binding the Head.

Routine II:

1. CONCEALING TO ATTENTION

Same as above. (Diag. C.6)

2. LEFT BOW STANCE WITH STAB

Left foot takes slanting pace to left front (N-E), knee bends to half squat, right leg straightens to form Left

Diag. C. 6

Bow Stance. At same time, right hand comes round waist and stabs straight forward, arm straight, shoulder following forward so focus of force reaches point. Left palm rests on right inner forearm, fingers up. Gaze forward. (Diag. C.7)

3. TURN WITH RIGHT BOW STANCE AND SLICE

a) Shift weight back. Right foot turns out, right leg

Diag. C. 7

bending slightly. Left foot turns in, left leg straightening. Torso turns round rightward to rear. At same time, right forearm turns inward, palm facing out, bending arm and raising sword, blade-edge up, point facing rear. Left hand rests on right forearm. Head turns right, gaze forward. (Diag. C.8.1)

Diag. C. 8.1

b) Torso turns slightly to left. Right leg bends forward, heel of left foot lifting off ground, leg straightening to form Right Bow Stance. At same time, right hand slices down forward, blade-edge down, point right. Left palm moves down to rear, bending at elbow and resting on hip. Gaze on sword-point. (Diag. C.8.2)

4. LEFT AND RIGHT WRIST SHEARING FLOURISH

a) Carry straight on from above. Right forearm turns inward, the "Tiger's Mouth" pressing tightly against sword handle, so sword-point faces down. (Diag. C.9.1)

Diag. C. 8.2

Diag. C. 9.1

b) Carry straight on. Right hand and wrist continue to revolve, so sword-point moves up, skipping past chest, and forward to form a straight arm Slice. (Diag. C.9.2)

c) Carry straight on. Right forearm turns outward, so right palm faces up, "Tiger's Mouth" pressing tightly against sword handle. Wrist turns down so sword-point faces down. (Diag. C.9.3)

d) Carry straight on. Right arm does not move,

Diag. C. 9.2

Diag. C. 9.3

right hand and wrist continuing to revolve, so sword-point passes outside the arm towards the back of the body close to the back, then up and forward to form a straight arm Slice. (Diag. C.9.4)

5. TURN WITH RIGHT BOW STANCE AND SWEEP THRUST

Raise left foot, toes turning out tc land in original

Diag. C. 9.4

place. Then, right foot takes large step over to left(E),
knee bending to half squat. Left foot straightens to form
Right Bow Stance. At same time, right hand follows
turn of body down and forward in a Sweep Thrust, blade-
edge up, point right, sword and arm forming a straight
line. (Diag. C.10)

Diag. C. 10

6. WRIST SWEEPING FLOURISH

a) Continue straight on from above. Right arm bends slightly, wrist bending upward, so sword-point sticks up, blade-edge inward. (Diag. C.11.1)

Diag. C. 11.1

b) Continue straight on. Right forearm twists inward, elbow turning up and over, so point of elbow faces up, and sword-point passes from above, close by the chest, then down and forward to form straight arm Reverse Sweep Thrust, blade-edge up, point right, sword and arm in a straight line. (Diag. C.11.2)

Diag. C. 11.2

c) Continue straight on. Forearm twists outward, "Tiger's Mouth" facing up, wrist continuing to revolve so sword points up, blade-edge facing out. (Diag. C.11.3)

Diag. C. 11.3

d) Carry straight on. Forearm twists outward, so "Tiger's Mouth" presses firmly on sword hilt, the other three fingers relaxing, hand and wrist revolving so sword-point passes towards rear, past outside of arm, close to back, then down and forward in a Sweep Thrust, blade-edge up, point facing right, sword and arm in a straight line. (Diag. C.11.4)

7. TURN WITH RIGHT BOW STANCE AND SLICE

Shift weight to left leg, Right foot rises with bent knee. Pivoting on left foot, torso turns 180° to right rear. Right foot lands forward(W), knee bending to half squat. Left leg straightens to form Right Bow Stance. At same time, right forearm turns inward following turn, arm rising, then falling in a straight arm Slice. (Diag. C.12)

Diag. C. 11.4

Diag. C. 12

8. VERTICAL BACK FLOURISH

a) Right leg straightens and torso turns to front to form Parallel Open Stance. At same time, right forearm turns inward, swinging with straight arm so sword swings down and left to front of stomach, blade-edge down, sword pointing left. (Diag. C.13.1)

b) Carry straight on. Right hand swings sword to

Diag. C. 13.1   Diag. C. 13.2

left then up from in front of stomach to above head, blade-edge facing up, point left, sword higher than head. (Diag. C.13.2)

c) Carry straight on. Right arm swings to right, arm straight at shouder level, sword and arm in a straight line. (Diag. C.13.3)

d) Carry straight on. Right forearm twists outward, right palm up, gripping sword hilt with "Tiger's Mouth" in pincer grip, the other three fingers relaxed, flourishing wrist with force so sword-point swings down, outside the right arm, past the back, up and to right in a Slice. (Diag. C.13.4)

e) Carry straight on. Forearm turns in, right palm facing rear, swinging down to right side with straight right arm. At same time, hold sword hilt with "Tiger's Mouth" in pincer grip, the other three fingers relaxed, spinning with force so that the sword-point swings down past back to behind right arm, palm facing rear, blade-edge left, point up. (Diag. C.13.5 and Rear View)

f) Carry straight on. Torso twists left. Right arm

116

Diag. C. 13.3

Diag. C. 13.4

follows turn of body forward, with bent arm rising, raising sword left, up and to right, so sword-point swings from behind back to right, then down and to left until horizontal in front of head, blade-edge up, point left. (Diag. C.13.6)

g) Carry straight on. Torso turns slightly to right; right arm stretching straight to right in a Slice. (Diag. C.13.7)

Diag. C. 13.5   Side View

Diag. C. 13.6

The three flourishes described above are essential basic broadsword skills which cannot be neglected. They must be thoroughly mastered. They can increase wrist flexibility and pincer grip strength, and are of use in the execution of many broadsword techniques and the rapid interchange of the various gripping techniques. They must, therefore, be practised repeatedly, developing from

Diag. C. 13.7

slow to fast until they can be done for a considerable time with ease and perfection.

Any one of these flourishes can also be practised individually over and over again. They are also called Level Flourishes. No matter which Flourish is practised the sword-body must be close to the right arm and body, its swing must be round, continuous and of even speed, and the movement of the waist must coordinate with it.

Chapter III
SINGLE BROADSWORD ROUTINES

Section 1
SMALL GROUPS OF CONNECTED MOVEMENTS FOR THE SINGLE BROADSWORD

Routine I:

1. Embracing to Attention
2. Bow Stance with Round the Middle Concealing
3. Empty Stance with Concealing
4. Bow Stance with Stab
5. Point Stance with Parry

Routine II:

1. Embracing to Attention
2. Bow Stance with Stab
3. Cross Stance with Backward Chop
4. Left and Right Side Press
5. Turn with Right Bow Stance and Slanting Slice
6. Point Stance with Parry

Routine III:

1. Embracing to Attention

2. Left Sweep Thrust
3. Bow Stance with Push
4. Knee Raise with Concealing
5. Horse Stance with Slice
6. Point Stance with Parry

Routine IV:

1. Embracing to Attention
2. Spin with Slap Kick
3. Knee Raise with Wrist Flourish
4. Crouching Stance with Concealing
5. Leg Hook with Jab
6. Point Stance with Parry

Routine V:

1. Embracing to Attention
2. Entwining the Head with Spring Kick
3. Rest Stance with Cut
4. Forward Sweep with Chop
5. Knee Raise with Hack
6. Point Stance with Parry

Routine I:

1. EMBRACING TO ATTENTION

Stand to attention facing South. Sword embraced in left hand, blade-edge outward, point up, sword-back very close to left forearm. Keep two arms slightly bent. Gaze forward. (Diag. D.1)

Essentials:

Legs straight, chest out, stomach in, head erect, neck straight. Sword vertical, sword-back sticking closely to left forearm.

2. BOW STANCE WITH ROUND THE MIDDLE CONCEALING

a) Raise arms up level in front of body, hands coming together, thumb of right hand spreading open, gripping hold of sword hilt. Gaze at right hand. (Diag. D. 2.1 and Side View)

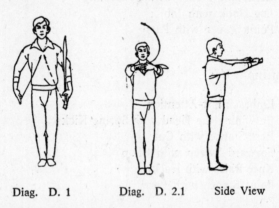

Diag. D. 1   Diag. D. 2.1   Side View

b) Right hand raises sword up and to left round left shoulder, sword-back close in to back, blade-edge out, point down. Left arm bends at elbow, left palm pulled in in front of right chest, fingers up, palm facing out. Gaze forward. (Diag. D. 2.2)

c) Right hand continues round past right shoulder, arm straightening out level to right side, sword and arm forming a straight line, blade-edge forward, point right.

Diag. D. 2.2

Left hand swings out level to left side in an arc, palm down. Gaze forward. (Diag. D. 2.3)

d) Torso turns to left. Left foot takes step forward (E), knee bending to half squat. Right leg straightens to form Left Bow Stance. At same time, right forearm turns in and swings level forward and to left, until the sword is close by the left ribs, blade-edge facing left, point to rear. Left arm rises up above head, palm up, fingers facing right. Gaze forward. (Diag. D.2.4)

Diag. D. 2.3

Diag. D. 2.4

Essentials:

The above four movements must be well coordinated, the Left Bow Stance and Concealing completed at the same time. When Entwining the Head, sword-back must stick close to body. During swings, right arm must be completly extended, point always down. The sword must be level when doing Round the Middle Concealing, right arm maintaining an outward curvature.

3. EMPTY STANCE WITH CONCEALING

a) Shift weight back, left leg straightening, torso turning right. At same time, right hand swings sword level from ribs to right side, blade-edge facing rear, point right. Left arm moves down to left side, palm down, fingers pointing out. Gaze on sword-point. (Diag. D. 3.1)

b) Weight shifts to right leg, right foot turning in. Left foot steps up to right instep, toes touching ground to form T-Stance. At same time, right forearm turns out and towards rear, arm rising up above head, blade-edge out, point down, circling round back to left and round to outside of left shoulder. Left palm withdrawn in front of right chest, palm facing outward, fingers up. Head turns left, gaze forward. (Diag. D. 3.2)

Diag. D. 3.1   Diag. D. 3.2

c) Torso turns slightly to left. Left foot moves forward, toes touching ground to form a Left Empty Stance. At same time, the right hand moves from outside left shoulder past torso to right, pulling sword back to form Concealing Stance, blade-edge down, point forward. Left palm pushes out from in front of chest to form Erect Palm, fingers up, side of little finger forward. Gaze on left palm. (Diag. D. 3.3)

Essentials:

The Empty Stance, Concealing and Palm Push must all be completed together. When Binding the Head, the sword-body must be vertical, the sword keeping close to the body, right arm raised up as far as possible. When Concealing, the shoulders should be pulled apart, left shoulder moving forward, right shoulder back.

Diag. D. 3.3

4. BOW STANCE WITH STAB

Left foot shifts forward(E), knee bending to half squat, right leg straightening to form Left Bow Stance. At same time, right hand stabs forward(E), blade-edge down, point forward. Left palm rests on inside of right forearm. Gaze forward. (Diag. D. 4)

Essentials:

Bow Stance and Stab should be completed together.

Diag. D. 4

Right arm must snap straight as it passes waist so the force reaches the point.

5. POINT STANCE WITH PARRY

a) Left leg straightens, torso turning 90° to right. Toes of left foot turn outward to form Parallel Open Stance. At same time, right hand swings sword down and to right side, level with shoulder, forearm turning outward so the blade-edge points down, point right. Left palm remains at left side, palm forward. Head turns right, gaze on sword-point. (Diag. D. 5.1)

Diag. D. 5.1   Diag. D. 5.2   Side View

b) Weight shifts to right leg, left foot pulled in close to right shin, then swiftly jabbing it down to front, toes touching ground(S) to form Left Point Stance. At same time, right hand raises sword up with straight arm, bending wrist to left so sword-body moves from right side to a horizontal Parry above the head, blade-edge up, point left(E). Left palm forms a Hook, straight arm stuck out to rear(N), hook point upward. Head turns to left, gaze forward. (Diag. D. 5.2 and Side View)

Essentials:

Parry above head, rear Hook, forward point of left foot and left turn of head should all be coordinated to finish together. The right wrist should snap swiftly and powerfully into the Parry. After the left foot has been raised in preparation for the Point Stance, it must first pass close to the right shin, then straightening the knee to jab down forward.

Routine II:

1. EMBRACING TO ATTENTION

Same as Diag. D. 1. (Diag. D.6)

Diag. D. 6

2. BOW STANCE WITH STAB

a) Same as Diag. 2.1. (Diag. D. 7.1)

b) Right foot does not move, toes of left foot turning outward, torso turning left. At same time, the right hand moves down and pulls sword back to form Concealing posture. Left arm bends at elbow, passing chest and thrusting forward in Palm Push, fingers up, side of little finger forward. Head turns left, gaze forward. (Diag. D 7.2)

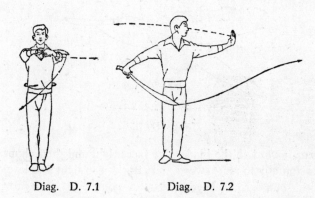

Diag. D. 7.1   Diag. D. 7.2

c) Left foot takes a step forward(E), knee bending to half squat, right leg straightening to form Left Bow Stance. At same time, right hand stabs straight forward (E), sword and arm in a straight line level with shoulder, blade-edge down, point forward. Left arm swings level to left then to rear, palm forward, fingers pointing left. Gaze on sword-point. (Diag. D. 7.3)

Essentials:

Stabbing arm must first be bent, then straightened out once it has passed waist so force reaches point. Stab and Bow Stance must be completed together, waist turning left, right shoulder shifting forward.

3. CROSS STANCE WITH BACKWARD CHOP

Right foot takes a step forward(E), toes turn outward, knee bending to half squat. Left leg straightens, heel rising up to form Cross Stance. At same time, right forearm

Diag. D. 7.3

turns inward so the blade-edge faces right and then chops horizontally to rear, sword and arm in a straight line level with shoulder, blade-edge to rear, point right. Left arm moves up, wrist slanting to form Exposed Palm, palm up, fingers pointing to right. Head turns right, gaze on sword-point. (Diag. D. 8)

Essentials:

When chopping to rear, waist must twist fully to right. Cross Stance, Rear Chop and Exposed Palm should all be completed together.

Diag. D. 8

4. LEFT AND RIGHT SIDE PRESSES

a) Torso turns left and tilts forward slightly. Left foot takes a step forward(E), toes turning out, leg slightly bent. Right leg straightens to form Cross Stance. At same time right forearm turns outward, bending wrist up so sword-point faces up, the sword swings up, forward and to lower left in Side Press, blade-edge down, point to rear. Left palm rests on inside of right forearm. Gaze on sword-body. (Diag. D. 9.1 and Rear View)

Diag. D. 9.1

b) Carry straight on. Right foot takes a step forward (E), toes turning out, leg slightly bent. Left leg straightens and heel rises in Cross Stance. At same time, right hand swings sword in an arc from lower left, up, forward and to lower right in a Side Press, blade-edge down, point to upper rear. Left arm straightens to upper left, palm up, finger to right. Head turns right, gaze on sword-body. (Diag. D. 9.2)

Essentials:

On both Left and Right Side Presses there should be

131

Side View

an angle between sword and arm, force reaching sword-back. The two Presses should be done in succession. Left Side Press should be coordinated with left step forward, Right Side Press with right step forward, twisting waist fully in Side Press, sword close to body, and moving in a curve. During Left and Right Side Presses, head and gaze follow movement of sword.

5. TURN WITH RIGHT BOW STANCE AND SLANTING SLICE

a) Carry straight on. Right foot leaps into the air, torso turning to right. Left foot strides forward(E), toes turning in so they face South as foot lands. Right foot follows behind left leg, landing to left(E) with heel raised to form Cross Stance. At same time, right hand moves up, forward and down in a Slice, blade-edge down, point to left and positioned outside left leg. Left palm follows leap and moves left, up and down to rest on right wrist. Head turns left, gaze on sword-body. (Diag. D. 10.1)

Diag. D. 9.2

Diag. D. 10.1

b) Carry straight on. Pivoting on the ball of the right foot and the heel of the left, turn 180° to right rear (chest now facing North). Right leg bends at knee, left leg straightening to form Right Bow Stance. At same time, following turn of body, straight right arm swings sword up and to right(E), blade-edge down, point to right(E). Left palm leaves right forearm and stops at right side. Gaze on sword-body. (Diag. D.10.2)

c) Carry straight on. Left foot takes a step forward (E, N-E), leg bends at knee, right leg straightening to form Left Bow Stance. At same time, right hand swings back, up and to right front in a Slice (S-E), blade-edge slanting down, point slanting up. Left arm follows Slice and swings up, forward, down and to upper left rear, palm up, fingers pointing right. Gaze on sword-point. (Diag. D.10.3)

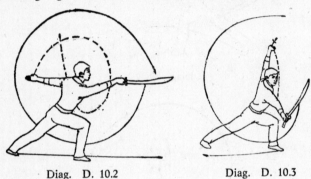

Diag. D. 10.2   Diag. D. 10.3

Essentials:

The three movements must be continuous. Sword swing must be circular, the swing of the arms coordinated. The Slice and Bow Stance should be completed together.

6. POINT STANCE WITH PARRY

Shift weight to right leg, torso turning right(S). The movements of Point Stance, Parry and Hook same as Diag. D. 5.2. (Diag. D.11)

Routine III:

1. EMBRACING TO ATTENTION

Same as Diag. D.1. (Diag. D.12)

Diag. D. 11   Diag. D. 12   Diag. D. 13.1

2. LEFT SWEEP THRUST

a) Same as Diag. D.2.1. (Diag. D.13.1.)

b) Feet do not move. Right hand swings sword up and to right side, blade-edge down, point right. Left arm bends, palm brought in in front of right chest, palm down. Head turns right, gaze on sword-point. (Diag. D.13.2)

c) Carry straight on. Torso turns left, left foot takes

Diag. D. 13.2

a step forward(E), toes turned outward. Right foot immediately takes a step forward(E), knee bending to half squat, left leg straightening to form Right Bow Stance. At same time, right hand swings sword with straight arm down and forward in a Sweep Thrust, blade-edge up, point forward at knee height. Left arm swings down, forward, up and back to left side, palm facing forward, fingers slanting up. Gaze on blade-edge. (Diag.D.13.3)

Diag. D. 13.3

Essentials:

Movements must be continuous. Bow Stance, Sweep Thrust and backward swing of left palm must all be completed together. The sword must move in an arc, keeping close to the body.

3. BOW STANCE WITH PUSH

a) Shift weight to left leg, torso turning right to face East. Right foot rises and with toes turned out, stamps down beside left instep. Leg bends, left leg rising as one stamps, top of foot hooking in behind right knee. At same time, right hand raises sword up, back and down with bent arm to left side, blade-edge pointing forward, point down. Left palm swings down, sword-back resting between thumb and forefinger, palm facing out, fingers to left. Gaze on sword-body. (Diag.D.14.1)

Diag. D. 14.1

b) Carry straight on. Left foot takes a step forward (E), knee bending to half squat, right leg straightening to form Left Bow Stance. At same time, right and left arms extend in a forward Push, blade-edge forward, point down. Gaze on sword-body. (Diag.D.14.2)

Diag. D. 14.2

Essentials:

The two movements must be continuous. The Stamp with right foot must be with the whole sole of the foot, powerful and with a clear sound. With the Push the torso should tilt forward slightly, pushing with all one's force.

4. KNEE RAISE WITH CONCEALING

a) Left leg straightens, torso turning right to face South, feet forming Parallel Open Stance. At same time right hand swings sword horizontally to right at shoulder height, so blade-edge faces rear and point right. Left hand leaves sword-back and extends straight out to left side of body. Gaze forward. (Diag.D.15.1)

b) Pivoting on left foot, feet turn in, torso turning to right rear(N-W), right foot retreating back a step(E), so as to form a Front-back Open Stance. Following turn of torso, right hand raises sword up and towards back in a Binding the Head movement, blade-edge facing rear, point down. Left palm is drawn in in front of right chest. Gaze forward. (Diag. D.15.2)

Diag. D. 15.1

Diag. D. 15.2

c) Shift weight to right leg, raising left knee up in front of body to form a Knee Raise Balance. At same time, right hand carries on round left shoulder, past front of body, down and then pulled to rear in Concealing position, blade-edge down, point forward. Left palm thrusts out forward, edge of little finger forward. Gaze forward. (Diag.D.15.3)

Essentials:

The movements must be continuous. Knee Raise, Palm Push and Concealing must all be completed together.

5. HORSE STANCE WITH SLICE

Left foot lands forward on ground(W), toes turned out. Right foot immediately takes a step forward(W), toes turned in, torso turning to left to face South, legs bending to half squat to form Horse Stance. At same time, right hand swings sword back, up and to right in a Slice, blade-edge facing lower right, point to upper right. Left arm moves down then up, slanting the wrist to turn the palm up in Exposed Palm, fingers pointing right. Head turns to right, gaze on sword-point. (Diag. D.16)

Diag. D. 15.3

Diag. D. 16

Essentials:

Right hand starts to move as soon as left foot touches ground. When right foot steps forward, sword swings up. The half squat to Horse Stance, Slice and Exposed Palm must all be completed together. Sword and arm should form an angle of about 90°, force reaching blade-edge.

6. POINT STANCE WITH PARRY

Straighten legs and shift weight on to right leg. Movements of Point Stance, Parry and Hook same as in Diag. D.5.2. (Diag. D.17)

Routine IV:

1. EMBRACING TO ATTENTION

Same as Diag. D.1. (Diag. D.18)

2. SPIN WITH SLAP KICK

a) Same as Diag. 2.1. (Diag. D.19.1)

Diag. D. 17   Diag. D. 18   Diag. D. 19.1

b) Left foot takes a pace sideways(E), knee bending, following which, the right leg takes a pace left(E) past the back of the left leg, heel raised to form Cross Stance. At same time, left arm swings horizontally to left side, palm out, fingers up. Meanwhile, right hand follows left and swings sword horizontally to left, bending the arm so the blade-edge faces left, point up. Head turns left, gaze on left palm. (Diag. D.19.2)

c) Pivoting on ball of right foot and heel of left foot, spin round right 270° to face East, arms following spin swinging down and to right, right hand raising sword up above head, blade-edge forward, point up. Left arm is raised level at back of body. Gaze forward. (Diag. D.19.3)

Diag. D. 19.2   Diag. D. 19.3

d) Carry straight on. Left foot takes a step forward(E). Right foot swings up level with chin, toes extended. At same time, right hand swings sword forward, down and to rear, blade-edge facing rear, point down. Left palm moves up then forward to slap top of right foot. Gaze on right foot. (Diag. D.19.4)

Essentials:

Diag. D. 19.4

The movements must be continuous. When spinning round, the torso leans back slightly, chest facing up, arms swinging in arcs. Slap of the right foot must be crisp and accurate.

3. KNEE RAISE WITH WRIST FLOURISH

Carry straight on. Right foot lands forward on ground (E), leg straight, toes turned out. Left knee is raised in front of body to form Knee Raise Balance. Torso turns to right (S). At same time, right hand swings sword forward and up, forearm turning inward so blade-edge faces right, then continues to right until level with shoulder when forearm turns out so sword moves down, left, up and to right outside right forearm in a Wrist Shearing Flourish. After Flourish, sword and arm form a straight line, blade-edge down, point right. After Flourish is completed, left arm bends and palm is brought in in front of right chest, palm facing right, fingers up. Head turns right, gaze on sword-point. (Diag. D.20)

Diag. D. 20

4. CROUCHING STANCE WITH CONCEALING

Right leg bends to full squat, the whole body turning slightly left. Left foot lands on ground beside right instep, then extends out to left to form Crouching Stance. At same time, right forearm turns inward, wrist bending down so that sword-point is close to right knee, blade-edge down, point forward, to form Concealing position. Left palm, fingers facing left(E), thrusts along left leg and up, palm forward, fingers facing up. Gaze on left palm. (Diag. D.21)

Essentials:

Bending of right leg, left leg sliding out to extend to left and Concealing should all be completed together.

5. LEG HOOK WITH JAB

Right leg straightens, weight shifting forward, left leg bending to half squat, toes straightening forward. Right leg bends, top of foot hooking in behind left knee to form

Diag. D. 21

Leg Hook Balance.   At same time, right hand extends sword straight forward, wrist bending down abruptly, so sword-point sinks down in a Jab.   Left palm rests on right inner forearm. Gaze on sword-point. (Diag. D.22)

Essentials:

The Jab with wrist must be forceful, so force reaches sword-point, wrist slightly higher than shoulder. Jab and Leg Hook must be completed together.

6. POINT STANCE WITH PARRY

Right foot steps back to ground(W), weight shifts to right leg.   Torso turns to right.   Movements of Point Stance, Parry and Hook same as in Diag. D.5.2. (Diag. D.23.)

Routine V:

1. EMBRACING TO ATTENTION

Same as in Diag. D.1. (Diag. D.24)

Diag. D. 22

Diag. D. 23

Diag. D. 24

Diag. D. 25.1

2. ENTWINING THE HEAD WITH SPRING KICK

a) Same as in Diag. D.2.1. (Diag. D.25.1)

b) Body turns to left, left foot takes a step forward (E), toes turning outward to form Fornt-back Open Stance. At same time, right hand swings sword left around left shoulder to back of body with arm raised up in an Entwining the Head, blade-edge to rear, point down.

Left palm is brought in in front of right chest. Gaze forward. (Diag. D. 25.2)

c) Carry straight on. Shift weight forward, body supported by straight left leg. Torso turns slightly to left rear. Right heel rises. At same time, right hand moves sword from behind back, round right shoulder, on to right, forward and to left so sword back is close in to left ribs to complete a Round the Middle Concealing, blade-edge out, point to rear (W). Left palm rises left and up, palm up, fingers pointing right. Gaze forward. (Diag. D.25.3)

Diag. D. 25.2

Diag. D. 25.3

d) Left toes turn out. Right leg bends at knee and rises, foot stretched straight, springing out forward (E) at waist height. Gaze on toes. (Diag. D.25.4)

Essentials:

The movements must be continuous. Round the Middle Concealing and Spring Kick should be completed together. For the Spring Kick bend the leg first, then straighten it, so the force reaches the top of the foot.

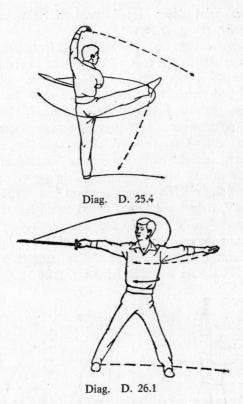

Diag. D. 25.4

Diag. D. 26.1

3. REST STANCE WITH CUT

a) Right foot lands in front of body, toes turned outward. Torso turns right to face South, following which
the left foot takes a stride to left(E) to form Parallel
Open Stance. At same time, right hand swings sword
forward and to right, until it is raised level out to right
side, blade-edge facing rear, point to right. Following
turn of body, left palm swings out to left side level with

shoulder, palm down. Head turns to right, gaze on sword-body. (Diag. D.26.1)

b) Carry straight on. Pivoting on left foot, torso turns right to rear(N), right foot taking a pace to right(E) to form Parallel Open Stance. At same time, following turn of body, right hand moves from right, back and up raising the sword in a Binding the Head, blade-edge to rear, point down. Left palm is brought in in front of right chest. Gaze forward. (Diag. D.26.2)

c) Carry straight on. Torso turns slightly to right. Left foot crosses behind right leg, landing to right(E), knees bending to full squat to form Rest Stance. At same time, right hand brings sword round left shoulder past front of body, to right and down in a Cut, blade-edge facing lower right, point forward. Left palm rises up to form Exposed Palm, palm up, fingers pointing to right. Gaze on sword-body. (Diag. D.26.3)

Diag. D. 26.2   Diag. D. 26.3

Essentials:

The three movements must be completed in succession, the Rest Stance and Cut completed together. The cutting right arm must be straight, pulling the sword slightly to rear.

4. FORWARD SWEEP WITH CHOP

a) Straighten legs, and pivoting on the right heel and ball of left foot, body turns right round leftward to face rear (S), forming a Parallel Open Stance. At same time, right hand moves forward and to left round left shoulder to rear, raising sword in an Entwining the Head, blade-edge to rear, point down. Left palm is pulled in in front of right chest, palm right, fingers up. Gaze forward. (Diag. D.27.1)

Diag. D. 27.1   Diag. D. 27.2

b) Carry straight on. Torso turns left to face East. Left foot shifts forward (E), toes turning out to form a Front-back Open Stance. At same time, right hand brings sword round right shoulder until extended level to right side, blade-edge forward, point right. Left palm swings out horizontally to left. Head turns right, gaze on sword-point. (Diag. D.27.2)

c) Carry straight on. Left leg bends to full squat,

heel raised. Torso turns leftward to rear. Extended right leg follows turn, sweeping forward and round for a revolution. At same time, right hand follows sweeping leg in a full horizontal sweep with blade-edge forward. Extended left arm follows body in a full horizontal turn. (Diag. D.27.3)

d) When the sweeping leg has completed one full turn, the torso turns to left(E). Weight shifts forward, left leg straightens and right leg bends up until foot is by inside of left knee. At same time, right hand moves sword past front of body towards the left, round left shoulder to rear, raising it up to perform an Entwining the Head, blade-edge to rear, point down. Left palm is pulled in in front of right chest, palm facing right, fingers up. Gaze forward. (Diag. D.27.4)

Diag. D. 27.3   Daig. D. 27.4

e) Carry straight on. Right foot takes a step forward (E), knee bending to half squat. Left leg straightens to form Right Bow Stance. At same time, right hand swings sword round right shoulder to right and forward in a Horizontal Chop, blade-edge facing left, point forward.

Diag. D. 27.5

Left palm swings horizontally out to left side, palm forward, fingers left. Gaze on sword-point. (Diag. D.27.5)

Essentials:

The five movements must be continuous. The Forward Leg Sweep must be straight because the right leg is led round by the waist. The toes should be pulled in during the Sweep, the foot not leaving the ground. As the sweep nears its completion, gradually bring the leg in so the feet become closer together.

5. KNEE RAISE WITH HACK

a) Right foot takes a step back(W), toes turned out, knee bending slightly, left leg straightening. Torso turns right to face South. At same time, right forearm turns in, pulling sword to right in front of chest with bent arm. Left palm moves in from left side and rests on right wrist which bends so sword rests on left arm, blade-edge pointing left, point to rear. Gaze on sword-body. (Diag. D.28.1)

b) Right leg straightens and takes all the weight. Left leg rises in front of body to form Knee Raise Balance.

Diag. D. 28.1   Diag. D. 28.2

At same time, right arm hacks to lower right (S-W), blade-edge facing rear, point down. Left palm rises up above head, palm up, fingers right. Gaze on sword-point. (Diag. D.28.2)

Essentials:

Hack and Knee Raise should be completed together. The Hack must be strong so force reaches blade-edge.

6. POINT STANCE WITH PARRY

Left foot lands forward(S). Point Stance, Parry and Hook same as Diag. 5.2. (Diag. D.29)

Diag. D. 29

Section 2

TITLES OF MOVEMENTS OF THE ELEMENTARY SINGLE BROADSWORD ROUTINE

Starting Posture

1. Embracing to Attention
2. Point Stance with Embracing and Exposed Palm

Part I

1. Cross Stance and Spin with Forward Slap Kick
2. Turn with Flying Step, Empty Stance with Concealing
3. Bow Stance with Stab
4. Sweep Thrust, Stamp and Push
5. Turn with Vertical Slash, Bow Stance with Slanting Slice
6. Covering Step with Slice, Knee Raise Parry
7. Side Press, Horse Stance with Slice
8. Cross Stance with Binding the Head, Rest Stance with Downward Cut
9. Sweep Thrust, Knee Raise Parry
10. Rest Stance with Downward Stab
11. Turn with Entwining the Head, Mid-air Heel Kick
12. Turn with Bow Stance and Side Parry

Part II

13. Left Side Press, Right Side Press
14. Leap to Cross Stance with Press
15. Turn to Jump, Crouching Stance with Concealing

16. Bow Stance with Stab
17. Entwining the Head with Turn and Inward Kick
18. Covering Step with Slice
19. Rest Stance with Concealing
20. Turn to Knee Raise with Stab
21. Bow Stance with Concealing, Change Step with Stab
22. T-Stance with Concealing
23. Bow Stance with Chop
24. Knee Raise with Downward Hack

Explanation of the Movements

Starting Posture:

1. EMBRACING TO ATTENTION

Face South standing to attention, sword embraced in left hand, blade-edge forward, point up. Right hand hangs at right side. Gaze level to front. (Diag. E.1)
Essentials:

Diag. E. 1

Chest out, stomach in, waist erect, head, neck and legs straight.

2. POINT STANCE WITH EMBRACING AND EXPOSED PALM

a) Torso turns slightly to right, right foot taking a pace to right front(S-W), leg slightly bent. At same time, left arm embracing sword extends out to front(S-W), blade-edge up, point to rear. Right arm bends, right palm brought in to waist, palm forward, fingers down. Gaze on sword-hilt. (Diag. E.2.1)

b) Raise left foot, stretching out foot and placing it in front of right foot, toes touching ground(S). Torso turns slightly to left. At same time, left arm bends and is pulled back to left side, blade-edge forward, point up. Right palm thrusts up above head, palm up, finger pointing left. Head turns left, gaze forward. (Diag. E. 2.2 and Side View)

Essentials:

Right step forward, extension of left arm forward and movement of right palm to waist should all be finished

Diag. E. 2.1   Diag. E. 2.2   Side View

together. Left arm should be extended as far and straight as possible, waist twisting to right, torso maintaining stuck out chest, etc. Point Stance, Embracing and upward thrust of palm should all be coordinated. Both legs should be straight for the Point Stance, weight shifting slightly forward.

Part I

1. CROSS STANCE AND SPIN WITH FORWARD SLAP KICK

a) Left foot takes a pace sideways to left(E), knee bending to half squat. Right foot passes behind left, taking a step to left(E), leg straight, ball of foot on ground to form Cross Stance. At same time, left arm swings up a position slightly higher than shoulder, blade-edge up, point to right. Right palm moves down past right side to in front of chest, palm left, fingers up. Gaze in direction of sword-hilt. (Diag. E.3.1)

b) Carry straight on. Torso turns to right rear(N). Right leg bends, left leg straightens. At same time, both

Diag. E. 3.1

Diag. E. 3.2   Diag. E. 3.3

arms swing down and to right, left arm stopping at left side, blade-edge up, point right, right arm continuing up, palm forward, fingers up. Gaze on right palm. (Diag. E. 3.2)

c) Left foot takes a step forward to right(E), knee bending slightly, feet in Front-back Open Stance, weight shifting forward. Right heel is raised. At same time, left arm rises up, raised level in front of torso, blade-edge up, point rear. Right palm swings forward, down, back and slanting up to behind head, palm forward, fingers up. Gaze forward. (Diag. E.3.3)

d) Right foot leaves ground, foot stretched out, swinging straight forward and up with leg straight, right palm swinging down from above to slap face of right foot. At same time, left arm swings to left rear, blade-edge forward, point up. Gaze on right palm. (Diag. E.3.4.)

Essentials:

The cross to rear of right foot should be stretched far, torso remaining erect. Cross Stance and swing of arms should be completed together. The spin should be fast,

Diag. E. 3.4

the swing of the arms coordinated and in a circle. The Slap Kick should be accurate and crisp, the leg swung up straight.

2. TURN WITH FLYING STEP, EMPTY STANCE WITH CONCEALING

a) Right foot lands back behind body(W). Left leg bending to half squat, right leg straightening to form Left Bow Stance. At same time, left arm rises up level to front, blade-edge up, sword point to rear. Right palm moves down to grasp sword-hilt. (Diag. E. 4.1)

b) Torso turns 180° to right rear, weight shifting to right leg(W), left foot raised up. At same time, straight right arm swings sword level to right, blade-edge right, point forward. Left arm is raised level at side, palm down. Gaze on sword-point. (Diag. E. 4.2)

c) Carry straight on. Right foot leaps off ground. Torso turns 180° to right rear(E), left leg, following turn of body, swings from rear and lands on ground(E) with

Diag. E. 4.1

toes turned in, leg slightly bent. Right leg swings to rear(W). At same time, right hand continues Level Swing of sword to right, blade-edge to right, point forward. Left arm follows body in a Level Swing, raised level at left side, palm down. Gaze on sword-point. (Diag. E. 4.3)

d) Carry straight on. Right foot lands behind body (W). Left foot is withdrawn to right instep, toes touching ground to form T-Stance. At same time, right arm swings right and to rear, raising sword to perform a Bind-

Diag. E. 4.2

Diag. E. 4.3

ing the Head, blade-edge to rear, point down. Left palm is withdrawn in from left side to in front of right chest, palm facing right, fingers up. Head turns to left(E), gaze forward. (Diag. E. 4.4)

Diag. E. 4.4

e) Carry straight on. Right leg bends to half squat, left foot shifting forward(E), leg slightly bent, toes touching ground to form Left Empty Stance. At same time, right hand comes round left shoulder, past front of body, down and then pulls sword to rear in Concealing position, blade-edge down, point forward. Left palm pushes out forward, fingers up, edge of little finger forward. Gaze on left hand. (Diag. E.4.5)

Essentials:

The distance of the turn and Flying Step can be more than one large pace. When leaping the swing of the sword must be on a level curve.

3. BOW STANCE WITH STAB

Left foot shifts forward(E), knee bending to half squat, right leg straightening to form Left Bow Stance. At same time, right hand stabs sword forward horizontally, blade-

Diag. E. 4.5

Diag. E. 5

edge down, point forward. Left palm rests on right wrist.
Gaze on sword-point. (Diag. E. 5)

Essentials:

Left Bow Stance and Stab must be completed together.
Stab must be powerful, so force reaches point.

4. SWEEP THRUST, STAMP AND PUSH

a) Shift weight back, torso turning to right(S), right

leg slightly bent, left leg drawn in to right instep, toes touching ground. At same time, right forearm turns inward, moving up and to right with straight arm so sword is at right side, blade-edge facing right, point up. Left palm extends straight up, palm up, fingers pointing right. Head turns right, gaze forward. (Diag. E. 6.1)

Diag. E. 6.1

b) Carry straight on. Torso turns left. Left foot takes a step to front left (E, S-E), toes turned out. Right foot then takes a step forward in same direction, knee bending to half squat, left leg extending to form Right Bow Stance. At same time, following step of right foot, right hand swings sword round to front in a Sweep Thrust at knee height, blade-edge up, point forward. Left palm swings to left side of body, palm forward, fingers left. Gaze on sword-point. (Diag. E. 6.2)

c) Torso turns left to face North. Weight shifts to left leg which bends at knee. Right foot is pulled in to left instep but does not touch ground. At same time, right hand moves up, arm bending in so sword-point turns to rear then down, stopping in front of chest, the arm at shoulder height, palm facing out, blade-edge forward and

Diag. E. 6.2

Diag. E. 6.3　Rear View

point down. Left palm rests on sword-back. Gaze forward. (Diag. E. 6.3 and Rear View)

d) Carry straight on. Right foot stamps down by left instep, toes turned out, torso turning right (E). Left foot takes a step forward(E), knee bending to half squat, right leg extending to form Left Bow Stance. At same time, both arms extend forward, blade-edge forward, point down to form Upright Push. Gaze on sword-body. (Diag. E. 6.4)

Essentials:

163

Diag. E. 6.4   Diag. E. 7.1

Sword must remain close to body during Sweep Thrust. Stamp must be at left instep, the whole foot connecting with the ground, powerful and crisp. The Push and Left Bow Stance should be completed together.

5. TURN WITH VERTICAL SLASH, BOW STANCE WITH SLANTING SLICE

a) Left leg straightens, weight shifting to right leg, leg bending slightly, torso turning to right rear. At same time, right arm rises to bring sword right and back behind head, blade-edge to rear, point to lower left. Left palm is pulled in to in front of right shoulder, palm facing right, fingers up. Head turns left, gaze forward. (Diag. E. 7.1)

b) Right foot pushes off ground, raising leg so left leg supports body. At same time, right hand brings sword round left shoulder, past front of body to right in a Vertical Slash, blade-edge facing right, point down. Left palm rests on right wrist. Gaze on sword-body. (Diag. E. 7.2)

Diag. E. 7.2   Diag. E. 7.3

c) Carry straight on. Using the force of the rightward swing of the Vertical Slash, spin round a full turn to the right, pivoting on the ball of the left foot. During the turn, right arm is extended straight at shoulder height, sword-point down, blade-edge out. Left palm rests on right wrist. Gaze on sword-body. (Diag. E.7.3)

d) Right foot stamps down by left instep, leg bending slightly, toes turned out. As right foot touches ground, left foot rises up and is hooked in behind right knee. At same time, right forearm turns outward, extending sword level to right side, blade-edge up, sword-point right. Left palm rests on right forearm, palm down. Gaze on sword-point. (Diag. E. 7.4)

e) Torso turns to left rear. Left foot takes a step forward (E, N-E), leg bending to half squat, right leg extending to form Left Bow Stance. At same time, right hand swings sword up and forward (E, N-E) in a Slice, blade-edge facing lower front, sword-point to upper front. Left palm swings down, left and up into an Exposed Palm, palm up, finger pointing right. Gaze on sword-point. (Diag. E. 7.5)

Diag. E. 7.4   Diag. E. 7.5

Essentials:

The shifts of weight to right and left before the turn
and Vertical Slash must be clear, the shifting of weight
to left and Binding the Head coming past the left shoulder
must be powerful and quick so as to provide enough momentum for the turn. The turn should also gain momentum
from the spring off by the right foot and the fierce twisting of the waist, carrying with them the right arm, and
in this way sword and strength will be united. During the
turn keep the back erect and head upright. Left Bow
Stance and Slice must be completed together.

6. COVERING STEP WITH SLICE, KNEE RAISE PARRY

a) Pivot on ball of left foot. Torso turns left, right
foot passes round in front of left leg to left in Covering
Step, toes touching ground and turned out to face Northwest. At same time, right arm swings sword down, past
outside of left leg to left, up, over, and to right in a Slice,
blade-edge down, point right. As sword swings past left

leg, left palm rests on right forearm, then as sword swings right in the Slice, the left palm rises up, palm facing up, fingers to right. Head turns right, gaze on sword-body. (Diag. E. 8.1)

Diag. E. 8.1

b) Torso turns to left rear(S). Right leg bends at knee, left leg straightens. At same time, sword follows turn of body in a forward Sweep Thrust, finishing straight out at shoulder height, blade-edge up, point right. Left palm swings down and out, extended straight at left side at shoulder height, palm down. Gaze on sword-point. (Diag. E. 8.2)

Diag. E. 8.2

c) Shift weight completely to right leg, left leg rising up with bent knee in front of body to form Knee Raise Balance. At same time, right forearm turns inward, arm rising up so sword parries horizontally above the head, blade-edge up, point left(E). Left palm turns to Hook, arm raised up slightly to rear, Hook pointing up. Head turns to left, gaze forward. (Diag. E. 8.3 and Side View)

Essentials:

Diag.　E. 8.3　　Side View

At same time as right foot executes Covering Step, left foot turns on ball of foot so the right foot lands facing Northwest. The swing of the sword for the Sweep Thrust, then up into the Parry must be unbroken and follow a circular path. There must be complete coordination of the upper and lower limbs during the Covering Step with Slice and the Knee Raise Parry.

7. SIDE PRESS, HORSE STANCE WITH SLICE

a) Left foot lands at left side(E), toes turned out to face North, knee bending. Torso follows in a left turn, right foot pivoting on ball, heel rising and leg straightening. At same time, sword with point leading swings to left, down and to rear in a Side Press, blade-edge down, point facing upper left. Left Hook turns to palm and rests on right wrist. Gaze on sword-point. (Diag. E. 9.1)

b) Right foot takes a step to right(E), toes turning in to face North, both legs bending to half squat to form Horse Stance(N). At same time, right hand raises sword up, then slices down to right, blade-edge facing lower right, point facing upper right. Left palm moves down, to left and up in Exposed Palm, palm facing out. Gaze on sword-point. (Diag. E. 9.2)

Diag. E. 9.1

Diag. E. 9.2

Essentials:

Left foot touching ground and Left Side Press should be completed together, waist twisting left at Side Press. The right step to Horse Stance, the Slice and the Exposed Palm should all be completed together. The swing of the blade from up to down in the Side Press and down to up in the Slice must be circular. The Side Press must be close to the body, head and eyes following the movement of the sword.

8. CROSS STANCE WITH BINDING THE HEAD, REST STANCE WITH DOWNWARD CUT

a) Torso turns slightly to left, legs straightening up but remaining slightly bent. At same time, right hand raises sword up, sword-point down, blade-edge pointing out, moving back and to left in a Binding the Head. Left palm is pulled in front of right chest, palm facing right, fingers up. Gaze forward. (Diag. E. 10.1)

Diag. E. 10.1

b) Carry straight on. Left foot passes behind right leg and lands at right side(E), heel raised to form Cross Stance. At same time, right hand brings sword round left shoulder, past front of body in a Hack to lower right, blade-edge facing rear, point to lower right. Left palm rises up to upper left, palm up, fingers pointing right. Gaze on sword-point. (Diag. E. 10.2)

c) Carry straight on. Torso turns slightly to left, right foot taking a side-step to right(E), leg straightening, left leg slightly bent. At same time, right hand raises sword to left and rear in a Binding the Head, blade-edge to rear, point down. Left palm is pulled in in front of right chest, palm facing right, fingers up. (Diag. E.10.3)

Diag. E. 10.2   Diag. E. 10.3

d) Carry straight on. Torso turns to right. Left foot
passes behind right leg and lands at right side(E), the legs
bending to full squat to form Rest Stance. At same time,
right hand brings sword round left shoulder, past front
of body to right and down in a Cut, blade-edge slanting
downward, point forward(N). Left palm rises to upper
left, palm up, fingers pointing right. Head turns right,
gaze on sword-body. (Diag. E. 10.4)

Essentials:

Diag. E. 10.4

The two Binding the Heads and the Downward Cuts must be completed successively. The Binding the Head and Cross Stance must be coordinated. The torso must twist to the right in the Rest Stance with Downward Cut, chest out and tilting forward slightly, sword pulled to rear.

9. SWEEP THRUST, KNEE RAISE PARRY

a) Straighten both legs. Pivoting on the right heel and ball of left foot, turn body 90° to left(W), right leg bent, left leg straight to form a Front-back Open Stance. At same time, right hand follows turn and raises sword up in front of body and round left shoulder in an Entwining the Head, blade-edge to rear, point down. Left palm is pulled in in front of right chest, palm facing out, fingers up. Gaze forward. (Diag. E.11.1)

Diag. E. 11.1

b) Carry straight on. Torso continues turn 180° to left(E). Left leg supports whole body, right knee raised up in front of body. At same time, sword swings round right side in a Sweep Thrust, blade-edge up, point forward.

Left hand rests on right forearm. Gaze on sword-body. (Diag. E. 11.2)

c) Carry straight on. Torso turns left(N). Left leg bends, right foot lands to rear(W), heel raised to form Cross Stance. At same time, right hand swings sword up and to left in a Press. Left palm rests on upper part of sword-back, fingers on top of back. Head turns left, gaze on sword-body. (Diag. E. 11.3)

Diag. E. 11.2   Diag. E. 11.3

d) Carry straight on. Torso turns right 180°(S), weight completely supported on right leg. Left knee rises in front of body to form Knee Raise Balance. At same time, right hand brings sword down, forward and up above head in a Parry, blade-edge up, point left. Left palm still rests on sword-back, palm up. Head turns left, gaze past left arm. (Diag. E. 11.4)

Essentials:

Full turn of body plus Entwining the Head, Knee Raise plus Sweep Thrust, Retreating Step plus Left Side Press and Left Knee Raise plus Parry should all be completed together. The paths of the Sweep Thrust, Press, and Parry should all be circular.

10. REST STANCE WITH DOWNWARD STAB

a) Left foot lands to front of body(E), both legs slightly bent. At same time, right hand pulls sword back, right
arm bent, wrist turned down, left hand still on sword-back
helping in Downward Press, blade-edge down, point forward. Gaze on sword-body. (Diag. E. 12.1)

Diag. E. 11.4   Diag. E. 12.1

b) Left foot turns out, weight shifting forward. At
same time, right forearm turns out, gripping palm up, and
situated in front of body, blade-edge facing left, point forward. Left palm moves up past front of body up above
head in a Parry, palm forward, fingers right. Gaze on
sword-point. (Diag. E. 12.2)

c) Carry straight on. Left foot springs off ground,
right foot leaping forward. Whilst in mid-air, right
forearm turns in and thrusts forward. (Diag. E. 12.3)

d) Right foot lands facing North. left foot landing
behind right leg, legs bending to full squat to form Rest
Stance (chest facing North). At same time, sword stabs
straight out(E), sword and arm in a straight line, blade-
edge down, point to right. Left palm is raised above head,

Diag. E. 12.2   Diag. E. 12.3

palm up, fingers pointing right.   Gaze on sword-point.
(Diag. E.12.4)

Diag.   E. 12.4

Essentials:
Left Footlanding plus Downward Press, and Rest
Stance plus Stab must be completed together. The leaping
pace forward by the right foot should be about the length
of a Bow Stance.

11. TURN WITH ENTWINING THE HEAD, MID-AIR HEEL KICK

a) Straighten both legs and, pivoting on balls of feet, turn body 90° to left (to face West), left heel landing on ground. At same time, right hand raises sword up in front of body and round left shoulder in an Entwining the Head, blade-edge pointing to rear, point down. Left palm withdraws to in front of right chest, palm facing out, fingers up. Gaze forward. (Diag. E. 13.1)

b) Carry straight on. Shift weight to right leg, knee slightly bent, left knee raised. At same time, right hand brings sword round right shoulder and forward to left side close by ribs to form Round the Middle Concealing, blade-edge out, point to rear. Left palm swings left and up, palm up, fingers pointing right. Gaze forward. (Diag. E. 13.2)

c) Carry straight on. Right foot leaps off ground, right leg bending in mid-air, toes pulled back. Left leg straightens naturally. (Diag. E.13.3)

d) Right leg straightens, kicking out forward. Left leg lands on ground. (Diag. E.13.4)

Diag. E. 13.1   Diag. E. 13.2   Diag. E. 13.3

Essentials:

Turn with Entwining the Head and mid-air Heel Kick must be completed successively. Complete the Concealing when raising left knee, complete kick when in mid-air. If beginners cannot execute kick while in mid-air, they can do it after landing or not perform the leap at all.

12. TURN WITH BOW STANCE AND SIDE PARRY

a) Right leg lands to rear with bent leg(E). Torso turns slightly to right. At same time, right hand swings sword forward and to right, blade-edge facing rear, point to right. Left palm swings down to left side, palm down. Gaze on sword-point. (Diag. E.14.1)

Diag. E. 13.4   Diag. E. 14.1

b) Carry straight on. Torso turns to right rear. Left foot takes a Covering Step forward (E, N-E), toes pulled in, right leg bent to form Bow Stance. At same time, sword and left palm follow turn of body in horizontal swing. (Diag. E.14.2)

Diag. E. 14.2

c) **Carry straight on.** Raise right leg. Pivoting on ball of left foot, turn 180° to right rear(N). Right foot lands at right side (toes to E, N-E), right leg bent, left leg straight. At same time, right hand raises sword up to right, blade-edge to rear, point down in a Binding the Head. Left palm is pulled in in front of right chest, palm facing right, fingers up. Gaze forward. (Diag. E. 14.3)

Diag. E. 14.3

d) **Carry straight on.** Right leg bends to half-squat, left leg extends to form Right Side Bow Stance. At same time,

178

right hand brings sword round left shoulder, past front of body to upper right in a Side Parry, blade-edge out, point to lower left, sword hilt at head height. Left palm rests on right wrist. Head turns left. Gaze forward. (Diag. E. 14.4)

Essentials:

All four movements must be completed successively. Right Side Bow Stance and Side Parry must be completed together. During Side Parry, right hand must use strength to bring sword up to upper right so force reaches blade-edge.

Part II

13. LEFT SIDE PRESS AND RIGHT SIDE PRESS

a) Shift weight to right leg. Left knee is raised up. At same time, right hand rises, sword not moving. Head turns left, gaze forward. (Diag. E. 15.1)

b) Torso turns 180° to left(S). Left foot lands forward (W) with toes turned outward, leg bent. Right leg

Diag. E. 14.4   Diag. E. 15.1

straightens, heel rising up to form Cross Stance. At same time, right hand swings sword with point leading forward, down and to left in a Side Press, blade-edge down, point to left. Left hand still rests on right wrist. Gaze on sword-body. (Diag. E. 15.2)

c) Carry straight on. Right knee rises up in front of body. At same time, right hand swings sword in a curve up and forward, blade-edge up, point facing out. Left palm leaves wrist, raised up above head, palm up, fingers pointing right. Gaze on sword-point. (Diag. E. 15.3)

Diag. E. 15.2   Diag. E. 15.3

d) Carry straight on. Torso turns slightly to right. Right foot lands forward on ground(W), toes turned outward. Left leg straightens, heel rising up to form Cross Stance. At same time, right hand swings sword down, to right and then rear in a Side Press, blade-edge down, point facing upper rear. Left palm still raised above head. Gaze on sword-point. (Diag. E. 15.4)

Essentials:

During Side Press, the sword-point should lead, moving in a circular path. The Left and Right Side Presses should be close to the body, so one should twist the waist accordingly to left or right. The Left and Right Side Presses should be coordinated with the step of the left or right foot into the Cross Stance. The gaze should follow the movement of the sword-point.

14.   LEAP TO CROSS STANCE WITH PRESS

a)   Carry straight on. Right foot leaps off the ground, heel raised backward. Left foot swings out in a big step sideways(W), leg straight. At same time, right hand raises sword up in an arc, blade-edge forward, point up. Left palm moves down slightly to left side. Gaze to left. (Diag. E.16.1)

Diag.   E. 15.4   Diag.   E. 16.1

b) Left foot lands, toes pointing North. Right foot passes behind left leg and lands to left(W), heel raised to form Cross Stance. At same time, right hand swings sword left and down to beside left hip in a Press, blade-edge down, sword-point to left. Left hand moves down to rest on right wrist. Gaze on sword-body. (Diag. E. 16.2)
    Essentials:

181

The distance of the leaping stride by the left foot should be equal to one Bow Stance. The rear cross step by the right foot should be well-stretched and completed at the same time as the Press. During the Press, the torso should twist to the left, though keeping the body upright.

15. TURN TO JUMP, CROUCHING STANCE WITH CONCEALING

a) Torso turns right(E). At same time, right hand leads sword in straight arm Sweep Thrust, blade-edge forward, point down. Left arm extends out to rear, palm down, fingers forward. Gaze on sword-body. (Diag. E. 17.1)

Diag. E. 16.2   Diag. E. 17.1

b) Carry straight on. Torso continues to turn right(S). Pivoting on balls of feet as torso turns, legs form Front-back Open Stance, right leg slightly bent. At same time, right hand follows body, swinging sword up and forward, blade-edge forward, point up. Left palm swings up above head, palm up, fingers forward. Gaze on sword-body. (Diag. E.17.2)

c) Carry straight on. Right knee rises up in front of body. At same time, straight right arm sinks slightly, sword not changing position. (Diag. E.17.3)

Diag. E. 17.2   Diag. E. 17.3

d) Left foot leaps into air, knee raised up. Right leg straightens, right foot landing close beside original position of left foot, leg slightly bent. Following, the left foot lands by right instep, toes touching ground. While the legs are in mid-air, the right hand performs an Upright Wrist Shearing Flourish outside the right arm. As the left foot lands, the sword is brought down by the right leg, blade-edge down, point forward. Left palm rests on right wrist. Gaze on sword-body. (Diag. E. 17.4)

e) Carry straight on. Torso turns slightly to right. Right leg bends to full squat, toes turned outward. Left foot extends out to left(W) to form Left Crouching Stance. At same time, straight right arm pulls sword right and to rear to form Concealing, blade-edge down, point forward(W). Left palm extends forward in Palm Push at shoulder height, side of little finger forward, fingers up. Gaze on left palm. (Diag. E. 17.5)

Diag. E. 17.4

Diag. E. 17.5

Essentials:

The five movements must be completed successively. The movement of the sword must remain circular throughout the whole process from Sweep Thrust to Concealing. The Wrist Shearing Flourish in mid-air must be fast and with a straight arm. Crouching Stance and Concealing should be completed together.

16. BOW STANCE WITH STAB

Shift weight forward, left leg bending to half-squat, toes

turning out, right leg straightening and toes turning in to form Left Bow Stance. At same time, straight right arm brings sword past waist forward in a Stab, ending at shoulder height, blade-edge down, point forwards. Left palm rests on right wrist. Gaze on sword-point. (Diag. E. 18)

Essentials:

Stab and Bow Stance should be completed together. The push off from the right leg must be powerful, torso remaining upright as one rises up.

17. ENTWINING THE HEAD WITH TURN AND INWARD KICK

a) Right foot takes a step forward(W), toes turned in. Torso turns left. Left toes touch ground by right instep, to form a High T-Stance (chest facing South). At same time, right hand moves left and up, raising sword to rear to perform Entwining the Head, blade-edge to rear, point down. Left palm is withdrawn in front of right chest, palm facing right, fingers up. Head turns left, gaze forward. (Diag. E.19.1)

Diag. E. 18   Diag. E. 19.1

b) Carry straight on. Pivoting on ball of right foot, turn body to face West. Left foot follows turn and takes a step forward(W) to form Left Bow Stance. At same time, right hand brings sword round right shoulder, past front of body to left, sword-back sticking close in to left ribs in Round the Middle Concealing, blade-edge out, point to rear. Left palm swings in a curve down, left and up above head, palm up, fingers right. Gaze forward. (Diag. E.19.2)

c) Carry straight on. Weight shifts forward, left heel rises, torso turns a little to left. Straight right leg swings forward and up, sole of foot turned in, bringing down left palm to strike right sole. Gaze on right foot. (Diag. E.19.3)

Diag. E. 19.2   Diag. E. 19.3

d) Carry straight on. After the contact, torso continues to turn left on ball of left foot, palm and foot separating. Following turn of body, right foot lands in front of left foot(E), leg slightly bent, left leg straight. Left palm rises up, palm up, fingers pointing right. Head turns right, gaze forward. (Diag. E.19.4)

Essentials:

The four movements must be continuous. The Entwining the Head and pulling in of left foot, the Round the Middle Concealing and step forward of left foot should be completed together. The slap of the Inward Kick must be sharp and accurate. During the Inward Kick the torso must remain erect, chest out, the foot kicking to head height. Do not bend the knees or waist or lower the head.

18. COVERING STEP WITH SLICE

a) Shift weight to right leg, toes turning outward. Straight left leg swings out to left side, foot extended straight. At same time, right hand swings sword level out to right side, blale-edge facing rear, point right. Left palm moves down to left side at shoulder height, palm down. Gaze forward. (Diag. E.20.1)

Diag. E. 19.4   Diag. E. 20.1

b) Carry straight on. Pivoting on ball of right foot, torso turns slightly to right. Left foot moves in front of right leg and lands at right side, toes turned outward. Right heel rises up. At same time, right hand brings sword up, at which point the left hand moves up to rest on right wrist. Next, both hands move down, so sword executes a Slice, blade-edge down, point left. (Diag. E.20.2)

Diag. E. 20.2

Essentials:

Swing of sword and turn, Covering Step and Downward Slice should be completed together. As sword swings up, left hand must quickly move up to rest on right wrist, then they continue on down together in the Slice. Waist should twist left with Cross Stance, torso maintaining upright stance.

19. REST STANCE WITH CONCEALING

a) Pivoting on heel of left foot, turn toes in. Pivoting on heel of right foot, turn toes out. Torso turns to right rear, Right leg bends to half squat, left leg straightening to form Right Bow Stance. At same time, straight right arm swings sword horizontally to right side in a Chop, blade-edge out, point forward. Left palm is raised level to left side. Gaze on sword-point. (Diag. E.21.1)

b) Carry straight on. Right foot takes a step to rear (toes pointing West), right leg bent, left leg straight to form Right Side Bow Stance. Torso turns right (to face South). At same time, right hand moves sword up and back to perform Binding the Head, blade-edge to rear, point down. Left palm is withdrawn in front of right chest, palm facing out, fingers up. Gaze forward. (Diag. E.21.2)

Diag. E. 21.1   Diag. E. 21.2

c) Carry straight on. Torso turns left, toes of right foot turn in. Left foot takes pace behind right foot(W), both legs bending to full squat to form Rest Stance. At same time, right hand brings sword round left shoulder, past front of body to right, pulling sword back into Concealing, blade-edge down, point forward. Left palm pushes out forward, side of little finger forward, fingers up. Gaze on left palm. (Diag. E.21.3)

Essentials:

The three movements must be completed successively. Rest Stance, Concealing and Palm Push should all be completed together.

20. TURN TO KNEE RAISE WITH STAB

a) Legs straighten, left foot takes a step forward, toes turned out. At same time, right hand raises sword back and up, blade-edge forward, point up. Left palm swings to behind body. Gaze forward. (Diag. E.22.1)

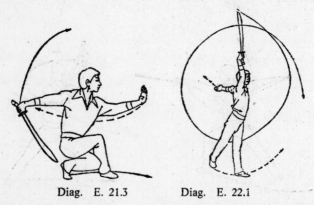

Diag. E. 21.3   Diag. E. 22.1

b) Carry straight on. Torso turns slightly left(N). Right leg swings out to right side(E), toes pointed. At same time, right hand swings sword right, down, to left, up and to right in a circle, blade-edge down, point to right. Left palm is raised level to left side, palm down. Gaze on sword-point. (Diag. E.22.2)

c) Carry straight on. Torso continues to turn left. Right foot passes in front of left foot and lands to left(W), toes turned slightly in. Left leg immediately bends, knee raised up in front of body. At same time, bent right arm stabs sword out horizontally forward past waist, sword and arm in a straight line(W), blade-edge down, point forward. Left palm rests on right forearm. Gaze on sword-point. (Diag. E.22.3)

Essentials:

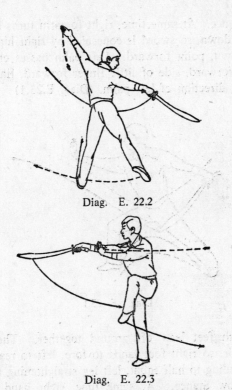

Diag. E. 22.2

Diag. E. 22.3

The three movements must be completed successively. The circular swing must be with straight arm. The Stab must pass waist in straight thrust forward, so force reaches sword-point. Knee Raise and Stab should be completed together.

21. BOW STANCE WITH CONCEALING, CHANGE STEP WITH STAB

a) Torso turns left. Left foot lands to fore(E), knee bending to half squat. Right leg straightens to form Left

Bow Stance. At same time, right forearm turns in, wrist turning down, so sword is concealed by right hip, blade-edge down, point forward. Left palm passes chest and pushes forward, side of little finger forward, fingers up. Gaze in direction of left palm. (Diag. E.23.1)

Diag. E. 23.1

b) Both feet leap off ground together. They pass in mid-air, so right foot lands to fore, left to rear, right knee bending to half squat, left leg straightening to form Right Bow Stance. At same time, right hand thrusts sword forward in Stab at shoulder height, sword and arm in a straight line. Left palm also stabs past waist to left side, palm forward, fingers pointing left. Gaze on sword-point. (Diag. E.23.2)

Essentials:

Turn of body to Bow Stance, bending of wrist to Concealing, Palm Push and turn of head should all be completed together. During the Leap and Change Step the feet should not be too far off ground, the Change Step fast and firm.

Diag. E. 23.2

22. T-STANCE WITH CONCEALING

a) Withdraw right foot to left instep, toes touching ground, both legs bending to half squat to form T-Stance. At same time, right hand swings sword horizontally to left, sticking close to left ribs to form Round the Middle Concealing, blade-edge to left, point to rear. Left palm rises up above head, palm up, fingers to right. Head turns right, gaze forward. (Diag. E.24.1)

b) Carry straight on. Torso turns right, right foot

Diag. E. 24.1

taking a stride to right side(S-W), left toes turned in, leg
slightly bent to form Open Stance. At same time, right
hand swings sword forward and to right, blade-edge to
rear, point right. Left palm moves down level to left
side, palm down. Head turns right, gaze on sword-point.
(Diag. E.24.2)

Diag. E. 24.2

c) Carry straight on. Left foot takes a step forward
to right side(S-W), toes turned in, leg slightly bent. Torso
turns right in accord (to face N-W), legs forming Open
Stance. At same time, right hand brings sword to rear
and up to form Binding the Head, blade-edge out, point
down. Left palm is withdrawn in front of right chest,
palm out, fingers up. Head turns left, gaze forward.
(Diag. E.24.3)

d) Carry straight on. Pivoting on ball of left foot,
forso turns round to right rear (S). Right foot follows
turn and takes a stride out to right side(S-W), knee bending to half squat, left leg straightening to form Right Bow
Stance. At same time, right hand moves round left
shoulder, past front of body, sword swinging horizontally
to right, sword and arm in a straight line, blade-edge

Diag. E. 24.3

Diag. E. 24.4

to rear, point right. Left palm straightens out to left side, palm down. Gaze on sword-point. (Diag. 24.4)

e) Carry straight on. Left foot steps up to right instep, toes touching ground to form T-Stance. At same time, right hand pulls sword right and back to Concealing position, blade-edge down, point to lower front. Left palm pushes out past waist(S-W), fingers up, side of little finger forward. Gaze in direction of left palm. (Diag. E.24.5)

Diag. E. 24.5

Diag. E. 25.1

23. BOW STANCE WITH CHOP

Left foot takes a step forward to left side (E), knee bending to half squat. Right foot straightens to form Left Bow Stance. At same time, straight right arm swings sword level to right side, the "Tiger's Mouth" of forearm swings horizontally to left and to back of torso to form Side Vertical Palm, palm forward. Gaze forward. (Diag. E.25)

Essentials:

The step forward of left foot, the withdrawal of hands, the Horizontal Chop and the palm turn to Hook must all be completed together.

24. KNEE RAISE WITH DOWNWARD HACK

Shift weight to right leg, torso turning right. Right leg straightens. Left leg bends, knee raised up in front of body. At same time, right forearm turns inward, sword hacking down to lower right(S-W), blade-edge to rear, point slanting down. Left Hook turns to palm, moving left and forward to rest on right forearm. Gaze on sword-point. (Diag. E.26)

Diag. E. 26

Essentials:
Left foot should spring off ground to add force to Knee Raise. Knee Raise and Downward Hack should be completed together.

CLOSING POSTURES

a) Left foot lands to side(E), torso turning slightly to left, legs evenly spaced apart. At same time, right arm bends at elbow, so sword moves to upper left, collected in in front of chest, resting slantwise across left upper arm, blade-edge out, point to upper left. Meanwhile, left forearm turns outward, palm turning up to grasp sword-guard. Gaze on sword-guard. (Diag. E.27.1)

b) Carry straight on. Pivoting on ball of left foot, turn a full circle to left rear. Right foot follows turn and lands back in original position(W), toes turned in, feet forming Parallel Open Stance. Left arm cradles sword in front of left chest, blade-edge out, point to upper left. Right hand releases hilt and stays by right side during turn. (Diag. E.27.2)

Diag. E. 27.1   Diag. E. 27.2

c) Carry straight on. Left leg moves in then extends out in front of right leg, slightly bent, toes extended and touching ground to form Point Stance. At same time, without sword leaving left upper arm, left hand swings up to left and down to form Embracing Position, blade-edge forward, point up. Right palm thrusts up right side above head, palm up, fingers pointing left. Head turns left, gaze forward. (Diag. E.27.3)

d) Left foot takes a small step to left, right foot then coming together with left. Left hand embracing sword does not move. Right palm drops down to right side. Head turns right, gaze forward. (Diag. E.27.4)

Diag. E. 27.3   Diag. E. 27.4

Essentials:

Body spin and left hand taking sword should be executed at the same time. Point Stance, downward movement of sword, Exposed Palm and head turning left should all be completed together. Concentration must remain full during Closing Posture, other requirements are same as Starting Posture.

Section 3

TITLES OF MOVEMENTS OF THE ADVANCED (COMPETITION) SINGLE BROADSWORD ROUTINE

Starting Postures:

1. Embracing to Attention
2. Embracing and Raising Fist

Part I

1. Left Slanting Slap Kick
2. Embracing with Turn and Leap
3. Bow Stance with Embracing and Palm Push
4. Knee Raise with Shoulder Back Rest and Exposed Palm
5. Embracing to Attention with Palm Push
6. Knee Raise with Embracing and Palm Thrust
7. Embracing with Large Leaping Step and Forward Thrust
8. Cross Stance with Embracing and Waist Spin
9. Stamp with Bow Stance and Embracing
10. Embracing with Point Stance and Exposed Palm
11. Knee Raise with Embracing and Palm Thrust
12. Striking Step with Embracing and Mid-air Flying Kick
13. Embracing with Full Squat and Ground Slap
14. Leap with Sword Exchange, Wrist Shearing Flourish
15. Crouching Stance with Concealing, Bow Stance with Stab
16. Cross Stance with Downward Hack
17. Retreating Step with Left and Right Sweep Thrust
18. Turn with Side Press, Horse Stance with Slice
19. Turn with Binding the Head, T-Stance with Parry

Part II

20. Right Sweep Thrust
21. Stamp with Sword Push
22. Cross Stance with Binding the Head and Downward Hack (three times)

23. Leg Hook with Wave, Stab to Attention
24. Left and Right Side Press
25. Forward Leap to Rest Stance wtih Downward Slice
26. Leaping Turn, Crouching Stance with Concealing
27. Bow Stance with Stab
28. Reverse Step with Binding the Head, Kneeling with Sword Push
29. Reverse Step with Binding the Head, Cross Stance with Concealing
30. Leaning Back with Stab
31. Binding the Head, Rest Stance with Downward Cut
32. Entwining the Head with Spring Kick
33. Covering Step with Brandish, Bow Stance with Side Parry
34. Turn with Entwining the Head, Inward Kick
35. Leaping Step with Wave
36. Knee Raise with Horizontal Chop
37. Crouching Stance with Upward Thrust
38. Leg Hook with Jab

Part III

39. Cross Stance with Reverse Sweep Thrust
40. Knee Raise with Concealing, Stab to Attention
41. Leaping Step with Downward Hack
42. Entwining the Head with Spin
43. Left Swipe
44. Bow Stance with Downward Stab
45. Turn to Bow Stance with Downward Stab
46. Turn with Downward Vertical Slash, Bow Stance with Concealing

Closing Postures

Starting Posture:

1. EMBRACING TO ATTENTION

Stand to attention facing South. Left hand embracing sword, thumb and "Tiger's Mouth" pressed against guard, index finger and middle finger gripping the hilt, middle finger, third finger and little finger supporting hilt so sword back sticks close to arm, blade-edge out, point up. Fingers of right hand together, arm hanging naturally by right side. Gaze forward. (Diag. F.1.)

2. EMBRACING AND RAISING FIST

a) Feet don't move. Right hand changes to Palm, rising up to upper right front, fingers pointing to right front. Left hand embraces sword without moving. Gaze on right palm. (Diag. F. 2.)

b) Left foot rises slightly, toes turning outward, heel close in to centre of right instep, torso turning slightly to left. Left palm turns to fist, forearm turning in, arm bending slightly so the eye of fist points down. Head turns left, gaze forward. (Diag. F. 3.)

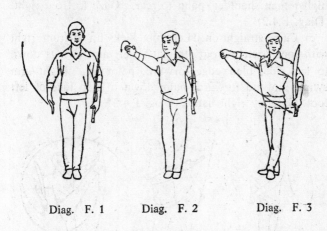

Diag. F. 1   Diag. F. 2   Diag. F. 3

Essentials:

The right arm should rise up slowly, and when it reaches about shoulder height the arm bends slightly and the palm turns to fist. As one makes the fist, turn the forearm inward. Bent right arm should form a curve. When position is fixed, stick out the chest, straighten the back, keeping the head up, gaze level and attention full.

Routine I:

1. LEFT SLANTING SLAP KICK

a) Arms cross in front of abdomen, right fist turning to palm on the outside, palm facing in. Gaze on right palm. (Diag. F.4.1)

b) Carry straight on. Right foot takes a step to right front (S-W). Torso turns slightly to right. Left hand swings left, up, right and forward to shoulder height, blade-edge up, point to rear. Right arm swings to left, up, right and to rear until it reaches right rear slightly higher than shoulder, palm to rear. Gaze to front right. (Diag. F.4.2)

c) Carry straight on. Left foot kicks up to front right with foot stretched out straight. Left arm swings down to left side, blade-edge forward, point up. Right arm swings up and forward, palm down to slap face of left foot. Gaze on right hand. (Diag. F.4.3)

Diag. F. 4.1   Diag. F. 4.2   Diag. F. 4.3

Essentials:
The three movements must be completed successively.

When crossing the arms, torso turns slightly to left. The arms must be straight when swinging, moving in circles and starting at the same time. The Slanting Slap Kick should be done with straight leg. The slap should be crisp and accurate.

2. EMBRACING WITH TURN AND LEAP

a) Carry straight on. Left foot lands in front of right. Following this, right foot takes a Covering Step in front of left leg to left (E), toes turned out, right knee bent, left leg straight, heel raised. At same time, straight right arm swings down and with straight left arm swings left, up and to right, left arm embracing sword in front of chest, blade-edge up, point to left. Right arm is raised level to right side, palm facing right, fingers up. Head turns right, gaze on right palm. (Diag. F.5.1)

Diag. F. 5.1

b) Carry straight on. Both legs bend at knees. Pivoting on balls of feet, torso makes a complete turn to upper left. At same time, left arm first swings left to form a straight line with right, then using the momentum of the turn, the two arms make complete circular swings. After the turn, the left foot is in front, leg bent to half squat. Bent right leg is behind left, foot to rear, heel raised to form Cross Stance. The arms finish extended out to sides, sword point behind back, right palm facing rear, fingers right. Left up head. Gaze forward. (Diag. F.5.2)

Diag. F. 5.2

c) Carry straight on. Right foot moves back to attention position, both legs bent to half squat. Arms do not move. Gaze forward. (Diag. F.5.3)

d) Carry straight on. Leap into the air with both feet, and whilst in mid-air, right leg straightens and left

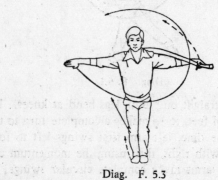

Diag. F. 5.3

leg bends up behind right. At same time, left arm bends and rises up, blade-edge to rear, point down. Right arm swings down, to left and up, slanting to upper right, palm up. Head turns right, gaze on right palm. (Diag.F.5.4)

Essentials:

The four movements must be completed successively. The leap and swing of arms must be simultaneous. During the spin, the position of the feet must not shift.

3. BOW STANCE WITH EMBRACING AND PALM PUSH

a) Right foot lands first, leg slightly bent. Left leg remains bent, face of foot hooking in behind right knee. At same time, left arm moves down and stops in front of chest, blade-edge up, point to left. Right arm bends down, palm swinging to behind right waist, palm facing out. Head turns to left, gaze forward . (Diag. F.6.1)

b) Carry straight on. Left foot takes a stride to left (E), leg bending to half squat, toes turned out, right leg straightening to form Left Side Bow Stance. At same time, left arm swings round to left side and then to rear,

Diag. F. 5.4   Diag. F. 6.1

back of left hand close to left side of waist, sword point facing upper left. Right palm swings forward, past front of left chest and to front right (S-W) in a Palm Push, fingers up, edge of little finger forward. Gaze on right palm. (Diag. F. 6.2)

Diag. F. 6.2

Essentials:

The two movements must be completed successively. As left foot takes stride to left and torso makes a slight turn to left, left arm swings behind body, and right palm is withdrawn to in front of chest. As left leg bends to Side Bow Stance, torso turns swiftly to right and right palm pushes out. One must emphasize the turn of the body first to left and then right.

4. KNEE RAISE WITH SHOULDER BACK REST AND EXPOSED PALM

a) Torso turns left (E). Following this right foot moves up parallel with left to form Open Stance, body standing erect. At same time, right arm bends, right palm brought in in front of left chest, fingers up, palm facing out. Left arm does not move. Gaze forward. (Diag. F.7.1)

b) Shift weight to right. Left leg rises up in front of body to form Knee Raise Balance. At same time, left arm rises up to left side so back of sword rests on shoulder, blade-edge up, point right. Right arm swings down, to right and up in an arc to above head, wrist slanting to form Exposed Palm, palm up, fingers pointing left. Gaze forward. (Diag. F.7.2)

Essentials:

The two movements should be completed successively. Knee Raise, Exposed Palm and Shoulder Back Rest should all be completed at the same time.

5. EMBRACING TO ATTENTION WITH PALM PUSH (TAKING 4 ARC-FORM PACES)

a) Left foot lands to right front (S-E), toes turned outward. Left arm is brought in in front of body, blade-edge up, point to left. Right arm moves down and out horizontally to right side, palm facing forward, fingers right. Gaze forward. (Diag. F.8.1)

Diag. F. 7.1   Diag. F. 7.2   Diag. F. 8.1

b) Carry straight on. Right foot takes a pace forward in front of left foot (S-E), right arm swinging slightly to rear, forearm turning in so palm faces rear. Left arm moves down slightly. Lower head, gaze on sword body. (Diag. F.8.2)

c) Carry straight on. Torso turns slightly to right. Left foot takes a step forward (E), toes turned out. At same time, left arm swings up and forward to about shoulder height. Right arm bends and moves down so fingers face down and hand is close to right hip. Gaze forward. (Diag. F.8.3)

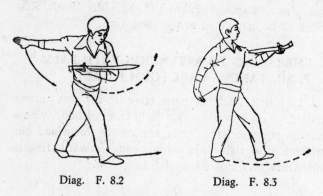

Diag. F. 8.2   Diag. F. 8.3

d) Carry straight on. Right foot takes a step forward (N-E), toes turning in slightly. At same time, left arm extends forward so hand is slightly above shoulder height, blade-edge up, point to rear. Right palm is withdrawn to right hip, palm forward, fingers down. Gaze forward. (Diag. F.8.4)

e) Carry straight on. Left foot moves up to beside right. Torso turns left to face Northwest. Left arm pulls down to side, blade-edge forward, point up. Right palm thrusts forward in Palm Push (N-E), fingers up, edge of little finger forward. Gaze on right palm. (Diag. F.8.5)

Essentials:

The four steps must be successive, making a half-circle, moving from slow to slightly quick. Swings of right and left arms must be coordinated during paces. Keep gaze on left arm during paces, but during Palm Push, gaze is in direction of right palm.

6. KNEE RAISE WITH EMBRACING AND PALM THRUST

a) Torso turns right. Left foot takes a step back (S-W), toes turned outward. Next, right foot takes a large step backward (S-W). At same time, left arm bends up and forward, palm down, hilt pressing down and forward at shoulder height, blade-edge forward, point to left. Right palm is withdrawn to right waist, palm forward, fingers down. Gaze on hilt. (Diag. F. 9.1)

b) Carry straight on. Weight shifts to rear, left knee rising up in front of body to form Knee Raise Balance. Torso turns slightly to left. At same time, right palm

Diag. F. 8.4   Diag. F. 8.5   Diag. F. 9.1

strikes forward above left arm in Palm Thrust (N-E), palm up and level with eyes. Left elbow strikes left so that hilt stops in front of right chest. Gaze on right palm. (Diag. F.9.2)

Diag. F. 9.2

Essentials:

Backward paces of left and right feet and concealed sword pressing forward must be completed together. Knee Raise and Palm Thrust must be completed together, right palm thrusting out from behind left palm.

7. EMBRACING WITH LARGE LEAPING STEP AND FORWARD THRUST

a) Torso turns left. Left leg extends straight out to left side (S-W), toes pulled in. Right leg bends to full squat to form Crouching Stance. At same time, following the extension of the left leg, left arm extends out in same direction blade-edge up, point to rear. Right forearm turns inward, palm facing forward, fingers right Gaze on sword hilt. (Diag. F. 10.1)

Diag. F. 10.1

b) **Carry** straight on. Left leg bends to forward bow. Right leg straightens. Body stands erect. Right foot takes a step forward (S-W), left knee raised up in front of body. At same time, left arm swings to rear past left side, blade-edge up, point right. Right palm swings up, then down past front of body to lower left by outside of left leg, arm extended straight, palm turned in. Waist twisted fully to left. Gaze to lower front. (Diag. F.10.2)

Diag. F. 10.2

c) Carry straight on.   Torso tilts forward   Left foot lands in front of right foot (S-W), then leaps powerfully off the ground.   Bent right leg leads, than both feet leap forward.   At same time, both arms swing up past front of body to above head.   Gaze forward. (Diag. F.10.3)

d) Right foot lands first (S-W), leg bending to full squat.   Left foot lands by right instep, sliding out straight to left side (S-W) to form Crouching Stance.   At same time, left arm first bends in in front of chest, then extends out in direction of left leg, blade-edge up, point to rear.   Right arm extends out to right side, palm down. Head turns left, gaze to lower front. (Diag. F.10.4)

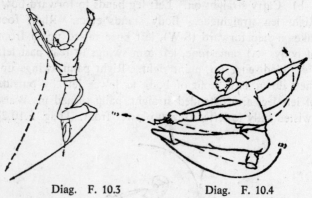

Diag. F. 10.3   Diag. F. 10.4

Essentials:

The four movements must be completed successively. Leap forward and swing of arms should lend momentum to each other, the leap being long and high. Torso should be straight during Crouching Stance.

8. CROSS STANCE WITH EMBRACING AND WAIST SPIN

a) Carry straight on. Right leg straightens, torso turns left (S). Following turn of torso, right leg takes a pace forward (W), weight shifting to right leg, left leg extending and swinging out to left side (about a foot off the ground), foot stretched out straight. At same time, right arm swings in front of body, arm bending so that centre of palm faces in. Left arm swings past front of body in an arc to left, slightly higher than shoulder, blade-edge up, point to right. Gaze to lower right. (Diag. F.11.1)

b) Carry straight on. Right leg bends to half squat, left foot landing to right rear (W), leg slightly bent, heel raised. At same time, both arms swing down and to right in arcs, bent left arm in front of chest, blade-edge up, point left. Right arm swings up level to right side, palm to rear, fingers right. Head turns right, gaze on right palm. (Diag. F.11.2)

Diag. F. 11.1   Diag. F. 11.2

c) Carry straight on. Pivoting on the balls of the feet, body spins a complete revolution to upper left. At same time, left arm first swings left so that it forms a straight line with right arm, then the two arms swing round in a complete circle following the movement of the body. After the spin, left leg bends to fore, right leg bends at rear, heel raised. Arms raised level to sides. Gaze forward. (Diag. F.11.3)

Diag. F. 11.3

Essentials:

The three movements must be completed successively. Knees should remain bent during spin, torso upright, arms straight and spinning in a circle.

9. STAMP WITH BOW STANCE AND EMBRAC- ING

a) Torso straight, right foot stamping down powerful- ly by left instep, leg slightly bent. Left knee bends, foot leaves ground and hooks behind right knee. At same time, left arm bends up and to right, coming down in front of chest, blade-edge up, point facing left. Right arm swings down, to left, up and to right, ending at shoulder height, palm facing rear, fingers right. Head turns right, gaze on right palm. (Diag. F.12.1)

b) Left foot takes a step to left(E), knee bends to half squat, right leg straightening to form Left Bow Stance.

Diag. F. 12.1

At same time, left arm swings down and forward (E) at shoulder height, blade-edge up, point to rear. Right arm bends and swings down and forward to inside of left elbow, fingers up, palm in. Gaze forward. (Diag. F.12.2)

Diag. F. 12.2

Essentials:

The Stamp should be crisp and powerful; the Bow Stance and swinging of arms should be completed together.

217

10. EMBRACING WITH POINT STANCE AND EXPOSED PALM

Weight shifts to right leg, torso straightening up. Left foot shifts to in front of right foot, toes touching ground to form Point Stance with both legs straight. At same time, left arm swings down, right past the body, up, left and down again to an Embracing position by the left side. Right arm swings down, right past body and up, arm straightening and wrist slanting to form Exposed Palm, palm up, fingers to left. Head turns left, gaze forward. (Diag. F.13)

Diag. F. 13

Essentials:

When straightening the legs, swing the arms; when swinging the arms lean back slightly. The Point Stance, Embracing, Exposed Palm and head turning left should all be coordinated well.

11. KNEE RAISE WITH EMBRACING AND PALM THRUST

a) Torso turns right (W). Left foot takes a step to

rear (N-E), immediately after which the right foot takes another step back (N-E). At same time, left arm swings left, up and forward, hilt pressing down, arm bent. Right palm moves down to right, pulled in by waist, arm bent, palm forward, fingers down. Gaze on back of left palm. (Diag. F.14.1)

b) Weight shifts back, torso turning slightly to left. Left knee bends and rises up in front of body to form Knee Raise Balance. Right palm thrusts out forward (W) over the top of left arm, palm up, fingers forward. At same time, left arm bends bringing hilt under right elbow, point to right. Gaze on right palm. (Diag. F.14.2)

Diag. F. 14.1   Diag. F. 14.2

Essentials:

Retreating steps and Hilt Press should be completed together; Knee Raise and Palm Thrust should be completed together.

12. STRIKING STEP WITH EMBRACING AND MID-AIR FLYING KICK

a) Torso turns slightly to left, left foot lands to left side (E), springing off as soon as it touches the ground, leaping up and forward. Right foot follows striking left instep. At same time, left arm swings horizontally past front of body to left at shoulder height, blade-edge up, point to rear. Right arm extends straight to right side, palm forward, fingers right. Head turns left, gaze forward. (Diag. F.15.1)

b) Torso turns slightly to left. Right foot lands first, left foot landing in front of right. Weight shifts forward, after which right foot immediately takes another step forward (E). Arms do not move. (Diag. F.15.2)

Diag. F. 15.1   Diag. F. 15.2

c) Carry straight on. Weight shifts forward, leaping off from right foot. Left knee rises up. (Diag. F.15.3)

d) In mid-air right foot Spring Kicks forward with foot stretched straight, right palm swinging forward to slap face of foot. Left arm swings up and then down to side of body, blade-edge forward, point up. Gaze on right foot. (Diag. F.15.4)

Essentials:

The movements from landing with Knee Raise to Striking Step with Mid-air Flying Kick should be continuous. The Flying Kick should be high, the slap crisp.

Diag. F. 15.3   Diag. F. 15.4

13. EMBRACIING WITH FULL SQUAT AND GROUND SLAP

Feet land together, legs bending to full squat. Torso leans forward. Right palm moves down to slap ground, left arm still by side. Gaze on right palm. (Diag. F. 16)

Essentials:

Full squat is essential. Hand slaps ground crisply in front of feet.

Diag. F. 16   Diag. F. 17.1

14. LEAP WITH SWORD EXCHANGE, WRIST SHEARING FLOURISH

a) Both feet leap off, knees bending in mid-air. At same time, both arms rise up above head, blade-edge up, point left. Right palm grasps hold of sword hilt. Head turns left, gaze forward. (Diag. F.17.1)

b) Having grasped sword in mid-air, right hand slices down to right rear, sword at shoulder height. Immediately after, right wrist executes a Wrist Shearing Flourish, spinning the sword right, down and to left close to right inner forearm, sword ending up to right, blade-edge down, point right. Left arm extends up above head with Exposed Palm, palm up, fingers right. Gaze on sword point. (Diag. F.17.2)

Diag. F. 17.2

Essentials:

As one leaps into the air, hilt must be grasped swiftly by right hand. Wrist Shearing Flourish must be performed at the highest point of leap.

15. CROUCHING STANCE WITH CONCEALING, BOW STANCE WITH STAB

a) Both feet land together, right leg bending to full

squat, left leg extending straight out to left side (E), toes pulled in, to form Crouching Stance. Right forearm turns in, wrist pulled in so sword moves down to form Concealing posture, blade-edge down, point forward. Left arm bends down in front of body then palm strikes out in Palm Push, fingers up, edge of little finger forward. Gaze on left palm. (Diag. F.18.1)

Diag. F. 18.1

b) Weight shifts forward, left leg bending forward, toes turning out, and right leg straightening to form Left Bow Stance. At same time, right hand stabs sword straight forward at shoulder height, blade-edge down, point forward. Left arm bends, palm resting on inner right forearm, fingers up. Gaze on sword point. (Diag. F.18.2)

Essentials:

Right leg must push off with force when changing from Crouching to Bow Stance, left leg bending at same time, not with body straightening up and then sinking down again. Bow Stance and Stab must be completed together.

16. CROSS STANCE WITH DOWNWARD HACK

Torso turns right, left foot taking a step back (W) and

Diag. F. 18.2

leg straightening. Right leg bends to half squat to form
Cross Stance. At same time, right arm swings right and
to lower rear in a Slanting Hack, blade-edge to rear, point
right. Left arm extends up above head with Exposed
Palm, palm up, fingers right. Gaze on sword point.
(Diag. F.19)

Essentials:

Diag. F. 19

Retreating step to form Cross Stance, Slanting Hack and Exposed Palm must all be completed together.

17. RETREATING STEP WITH LEFT AND RIGHT SWEEP THRUST

a) Torso turns slightly left, left foot taking a step forward (E), toes turned out, right foot then immediately taking a step forward (E), toes turning in to form Parallel Open Step (facing N). At same time, right hand rises up so sword point is down, moving forward and to left around left shoulder in an Entwining the Head, blade-edge to rear, point down. Left palm is withdrawn in front of right chest, palm facing out, fingers up. Gaze forward. (Diag. F.20.1)

b) Carry straight on. Toes of left foot turn out, torso turning 90° to left (facing W). Right arm swings sword right and forward in a Horizontal Chop, blade-edge left, point forward. Left palm moves down, left and forward to rest on right forearm. Gaze on sword point. (Diag. F.20.2)

c) Carry straight on. Right forearm turns out so

Diag. F. 20.1   Diag. F. 20.2

blade-edge faces up, then immediately arm bends up so that sword swings from left side of head back, down and forward in a Reverse Sweep Thrust with "Tiger's Mouth" down, so sword ends up with blade-edge up and point forward. Left palm accompanies swing of right arm still resting on forearm. Gaze on sword point. (Diag. F.20.3)

d) Carry straight on. Left foot takes a reverse step back (E), right leg bending slightly. At same time, right hand swings sword up past right side to rear, down and forward in a Sweep Thrust, palm up, blade-edge up, point forward. When sword moves up, left palm leaves right forearm, palm turning out and immediately swinging down, forward and up to stop above head, arm straight, palm up, fingers right. Gaze forward. (Diag. F.20.4)

Diag. F. 20.3   Diag. F. 20.4

Essentials:

The four movements must be completed successively. The horizontal Chop after the Entwining the Head must be clearly completed, however the sword does not stop before going on into the Reverse Sweep Thrust. Movement of sword during Left and Right Sweep Thrust must be circular, sword sticking close to the sides. Right Sweep Thrust, swing of left palm and step backward must all be completed together.

18. TURN WITH SIDE PRESS, HORSE STANCE WITH SLICE

a) Toes of right foot turn in, weight shifting to right leg. Torso turns left, toes of left foot rising up, turning out and then landing again (E). At same time, right forearm turns in, wrist sweeping up above head so blade-edge faces upper front, point lower front. Left arm bends, palm brought in in front of right chest, palm pointing right, fingers up. Head turns left, gaze forward. (Diag. F.21.1)

b) Right foot takes a step forward (E), both legs bending to half squat to form Horse Stance. At same time, right hand swings sword down, left, and up in a Side Press. When the Horse Stance has been completed, right forearm turns in so that the sword swings down to right side in a Slanting Slice, blade-edge to lower right, point to upper right. Left palm swings in an arc down, left and up to above head, where wrist slants to form Exposed Palm, palm up, fingers to right. Head turns right, gaze on sword point. (Diag. F.21.2)

Essentials:

The two movements must be completed successively. The Side Press should be close to the left side, the sword moving on a circular path from Side Press to Slice. Slice and Horse Stance should be completed together.

19. TURN WITH BINDING THE HEAD, T-STANCE WITH PARRY

a) Both legs straighten. Pivoting on heel of right

Diag. F. 21.1   Diag. F. 21.2

foot, torso turns 180° to right rear, left foot taking a step
forward (E) to form Parallel Open Stance. At same time,
right hand swings sword horizontally in front of chest
to under left armpit, point to rear. Left palm remains
above head. Gaze forward. (Diag. F.22.1)

b) Carry straight on. Right foot takes a step backward (E), torso accordingly turning right round to right
rear (N). At same time, right hand raises sword forward,
right and up behind back to perform Binding the Head,

Diag. F. 22.1

blade-edge out, point down. Left palm is withdrawn to in front of right chest. Gaze forward. (Diag. F.22.2)

c) Carry straight on. Left foot comes up beside right instep, toes touching ground, both legs bending to half squat to form T-Stance. At same time, right hand brings sword round left shoulder, past front of body to right and up, wrist bending so sword parries level above head, blade-edge up, point left. Left palm turns to Hook, moving left and to rear, Hook pointing up. Head turns left, gaze forward. (Diag. F.22.3)

Diag. F. 22.2

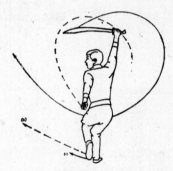

Diag. F. 22.3

Essentials:
The three movements must be completed successively. Binding the Head and right about turn should be completed together. T-Stance, Parry and Hook swing to rear should all be completed together.

Routine II:

20. RIGHT SWEEP THRUST

Left foot takes a step to left front (N-W), toes turned

out. Right foot follows with a step in the same direction, knee bending to half squat, left leg straightening to form Right Bow Stance. At same time, right hand swings back, down past right side and forward in a Sweep Thrust, arm at shoulder height, blade-edge up, point right. Left Hook turns to palm, swinging down, forward, up and back to left side, palm forward, fingers left. Gaze on sword-point. (Diag. F.23)

Diag. F. 23

Essentials:

When left foot takes step forward, sword and left palm start moving together. Right Bow Stance, Sweep Thrust and swing of left palm must be completed together. During Sweep Thrust, when sword is at right side torso should turn right accordingly. When sword thrusts forward, the torso should turn left. Sword and arm must be straight, sword keeping close to body and moving on a circular path.

21. STAMP WITH SWORD PUSH

a) Weight shifts to rear. Right foot rises up above left instep, then stamps down. Left knee immediately rises up, foot stretched straight and hooked behind right knee. At same time, torso turns left and right hand moves up, past left side to rear, down then up in front of body, right elbow bent at shoulder height, palm facing out, hilt up, blade-edge forward and point down. Left palm rests on sword-back. Gaze on sword body. (Diag. F.24.1)

b) Left foot lands forward (N-W), knee bends to half squat, right leg straightening to form Left Bow Stance. At same time, both arms extend forward in Sword Push, blade-edge forward, point down. Gaze on sword body. (Diag. F. 24. 2)

Diag. F. 24.1   Diag. F. 24.2

Essentials:

The two movements must be successively completed. Stamp and withdrawing of sword in front of left chest must be completed together. Bow Stance and Sword Push must be completed together.

22. CROSS STANCE WITH BINDING THE HEAD AND DOWNWARD HACK (THREE TIMES)

a) Torso turns right.   Right leg bends, left leg

straightens to form Bow Stance. At same time, right hand chops level to right side with blade-edge facing right. Left palm is extended level to left side, palm down, fingers left. Gaze on sword point. (Diag. F.25.1)

Diag. F. 25.1

b) Pivoting on ball of left foot, torso turns 180° to right rear (S-W). Right foot follows turn and takes a Reverse step back (N-W) to form Parallel Open Step. At same time right hand raises sword back to perform Binding the Head, blade-edge to rear, point down. Left palm is withdrawn to in front of right chest, fingers up, palm to right. Head turns left, gaze forward. (Diag. F.25.2)

c) Weight shifts right, left foot passing behind right, heel raised, to form Cross Stance (N-W). At same time, right hand brings sword round left shoulder past chest and hacks down to lower right, blade-edge to rear, point slanting down. Left arm extends up, palm up, fingers right. Gaze on sword point. (Diag. F.25.3)

d) Right foot takes a pace to right (N-W) to form Parallel Open Step. At same time, right hand lifts sword

up to rear to perform Binding the Head, blade-edge to rear, point down. Left palm is withdrawn in front of right chest, fingers up, palm right. Head turns left, gaze forward. (Diag. F.25.4)

Diag. F. 25.4   Diag. F. 25.5

e) Same as (c). (Diag. F.25.5)
f) Same as (d). (Diag. F.25.6)
g) Right leg bends. Left foot takes a step behind right,

heel raised, to form Cross Stance. At same time, right
hand brings sword round left shoulder, past front of body
and hacks to lower right (N-W) with straight arm, blade-
edge to rear, point to lower right. Left palm pushes up
above head, palm up, fingers right. Gaze on sword-point.
(Diag. F.25.7)

Diag. F. 25.6   Diag. F. 25.7

Essentials:

The seven movements must be completed successively.
Binding the Head and Parallel Open Step, and sword
swing and Cross Stance should all be well coordinated.
During the Cross Stance with Hack, the torso should
twist to the right as much as possible, sword and back
leg in same direction (N-W).

23. LEG HOOK WITH WAVE, STAB TO ATTENTION

a) Pivoting on the heel of the right foot and ball of
the left foot, body turns to left rear (chest facing N-W).
At same time, right hand swings sword left and forward
to in front of chest at shoulder height, blade-edge right,

point forward. Left palm rests on right forearm, fingers up, palm right. Gaze forward. (Diag. F.26.1)

Diag. F. 26.1

b) Weight shifts to left leg, which bends to slight squat. Right knee rises, foot hooking behind left knee. At same time, torso leans back, right arm bends slightly and the wrist revolves so that the sword completes a circular wave in front of the head. The arm is then withdrawn to in front of the abdomen, blade-edge left, point forward. Left palm follows Wave and remains on right forearm. Gaze forward. (Diag. F.26.2)

c) Right foot lands forward, left foot then taking a step up beside right to come to attention (N-W). Torso turns 90° to left. At same time, right hand stabs sword straight forward from the abdomen, sword and arm in a straight line at shoulder height, blade-edge down, point right. Left palm strikes straight out to left, arm straight, palm forward, fingers left. Gaze on sword-point. (Diag. F.26.3)

Essentials:

Wave must be level throughout, and when sword reaches head, lift up the head and lean back. The steps

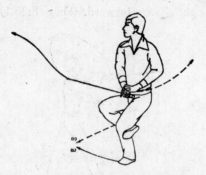

Diag. F. 26.2

forward and the Stab must be completed together. For the Stab to Attention the body must be twisted to the left as far as possible, arms stretched apart.

24. LEFT AND RIGHT SIDE PRESS

a) Left foot takes a step to rear (S-E), right knee rises up in front of body. At same time, right forearm turns in so blade-edge faces up, and wrist bends down so sword

Diag. F. 26.3

point is down. Then press sword down to left and to rear, point to upper rear, left palm resting on right forearm. Gaze on sword point. (Diag. F.27.1)

b) Right foot lands forward (N-W), toes turned out. At same time, sword moves up and forward, gripping palm turned in, blade-edge up and point forward. Left palm still rests on right wrist. Gaze forward. (Diag. F.27.2)

Diag. F. 27.1   Diag. F. 27.2

c) Weight shifts forward, left heel rises up. At same time, straight right arm sweeps sword forward, down past the right and to rear in a Side Press, sword and arm in a straight line, blade-edge down, point to rear. Left arm extends straight out to left side, palm forward, fingers left. Head turns right, gaze on sword point. (Diag. F. 27.3)

Essentials:

The movement of the sword for both side presses must be circular, the sword sticking close to the sides of the body. Side Press and footwork must be executed together, with a large movement of waist to left and right.

237

Diag. F. 27.3

25. FORWARD LEAP TO REST STANCE WITH DOWNWARD SLICE

a) Carry straight on. Weight shifts forward, right foot leaping off ground and torso turning slightly to right. Left foot takes a big stride forward in mid-air (N-W). Both arms swing out to sides. Gaze on sword body. (Diag. F.28.1)

b) Left foot lands with toes turned in, right foot landing behind left (W). Both legs bend to full squat to form

Diag. F. 28.1

Rest Stance. At same time, sword slices left and down, finishing by outside of left leg, blade-edge down, point left (N-W). Left palm rests on front part of sword back. Gaze on sword body. (Diag. F. 28. 2 and Rear View)

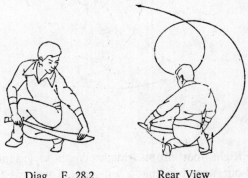

Diag. F. 28.2   Rear View

Essentials:

Movements **24** and **25** should be completed successively. Rest Stance and Downward Slice should be completed together.

26. LEAPING TURN, CROUCHING STANCE WITH CONCEALING

a)   Spring off ground powerfully with both feet, body turning to right rear in mid-air, knees bent. At same time, right arm follows leap and rightward turn of body and moves up until body has turned 270° (chest facing West and also the highest point of the leap). Then, with the arm extended straight, the wrist revolves so that the sword completes an upright Wrist Shearing Flourish outside the right arm. Left palm remains on right forearm throughout. Gaze forward. (Diag. F.29.1)

Diag. F. 29.1

b) Right foot drops straight down to ground, toes turned out, knee bending to full squat. Torso twists right. Left leg extends out to left side (N-W) to form Crouching Stance. Right hand pulls sword down, right and back to Concealing position, blade-edge down, point forward. Left palm pushes out forward, fingers up, edge of little finger forward. Gaze on left palm. (Diag. F.29.2)

Essentials:

Diag. F. 29.2

The leaping turn must be high, the right Wrist Shearing Flourish completed in mid-air. To form Crouching Stance, left foot must slide out on whole sole of foot to front from beside right instep, and must be completed at same time as Concealing and Palm Push. In Crouching Stance keep chest out, waist erect.

27. BOW STANCE WITH STAB

Left leg bends forward to half squat, right leg straightening to form Left Bow Stance. At same time, right hand stabs sword straight out to front, sword and arm in a straight line, blade-edge down, point forward. Left palm rests on right forearm. Gaze on sword point. (Diag. F.30)

Diag. F. 30

Essentials:
Formation of Bow Stance and Stab should be completed together.

28. REVERSE STEP WITH BINDING THE HEAD, KNEELING WITH SWORD PUSH

a) Left foot does not move. Right foot moves up a

half pace. Right arm bends so that sword sweeps left, sword back close in to left side of ribs to form Round the Middle Concealing, blade-edge to left, point to rear. Left palm parries above head, palm up, fingers right. Gaze forward. (Diag. F.31.1)

b) Pivoting on ball of left foot, torso turns right 180° (chest facing S-E). Right foot takes a step to rear (N-W). During the turn, right arm swings sword level to right, then to rear and up to perform Binding the Head. Left palm is withdrawn in front of chest, fingers up, palm facing out. Gaze forward. (Diag. F.31.2)

Diag. F. 31.1   Diag. F. 31.2

c) Right leg kneels on ground. At same time, right hand comes round left shoulder, past front of body, bringing the sword down horizontally, blade-edge forward, point left. Left palm moves down and rests on sword back, fingers forward. Gaze on sword body. (Diag. F. 31.3)

d) Torso leans back. With left hand supporting back of sword, push up and back with horizontal sword, blade-

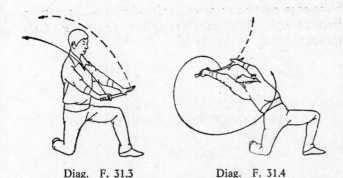

Diag. F. 31.3   Diag. F. 31.4

edge up, point left. Head leans back to look at sword. (Diag. F. 31. 4).

Essentials:

Turn with Reverse Step and Binding the Head should all be completed together. Kneel and backward Sword Push should be completed together. One must lift head and lean back fully and when sword rises up past chest it must not be too far away.

29. REVERSE STEP WITH BINDING THE HEAD. CROSS STANCE WITH CONCEALING

a) Legs straighten up and left hand leaves sword back, arm extended straight up above head, palm up, fingers right. Torso straightens, right hand swinging sword right, forward and left under left armpit, blade-edge out, point to rear. Gaze forward. (Diag. F.32.1)

b) Right foot takes a step to rear (N-W), left foot then taking a step in the same direction. At same time, right hand swings sword forward, right, backward and straight up above head to perform Binding the Head,

243

blade-edge out, point down. Left palm is withdrawn in front of right chest, palm facing out, fingers up. Gaze forward. (Diag. F. 32. 2)

Diag. F. 32.1   Diag. F. 32.2

c) Carry straight on. Left foot takes a step to rear (N-W), heel raised. Right leg bends to half squat to form Cross Stance. Right hand brings sword round left shoulder, past front of body to right, then pulling sword to rear in Concealing. Left palm pushes out forward (S-E), fingers up, edge of little finger forward. Gaze forward. (Diag. F. 32. 3)

Diag. F. 32.3

Essentials:

The three movements must be completed successively. Cross Stance, Concealing and Palm Push must all be completed together.

30. LEANING BACK WITH STAB

a) Left foot takes a step forward (S-E). Right foot steps up beside left to attention. Both legs bend to half squat. At same time, right arm extends straight out forward, wrist bending up, so sword springs up and back to above right shoulder, blade-edge up, point to rear. Left palm rests on right wrist. Gaze on sword body. (Diag. F. 33. 1)

b) Torso leans over backward. Left leg supports body while right leg extends out and up, foot stretched out (S-E). At same time, right hand stabs straight back (N-W), blade-edge up, point to rear. Left palm thrusts out in direction of kicking leg, palm facing right, fingers forward. Lift head, gaze on sword point. (Diag. F.33.2)

Essentials:

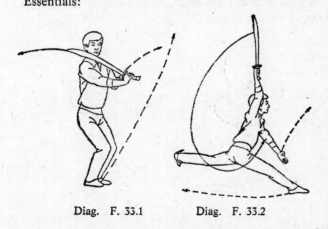

Diag. F. 33.1   Diag. F. 33.2

To execute the leaning back balance one must first make sure that the left foot is firm and when the weight is centred, then lean back and extend the leg. The stab to rear must be level, sword and arm in a straight line.

31. BINDING THE HEAD, REST STANCE WITH DOWNWARD CUT

a) Torso straightens up, right foot landing in front of body, leg slightly bent, toes turned out. Left leg straightens, heel rising up. At same time, right hand swings sword right, forward and left under left armpit, blade-edge out, point to upper front. Left palm extends straight up above head in Exposed Palm, fingers right. Head turns right, gaze forward. (Diag. F.34.1)

b) Left foot takes a step forward (S-E), right foot immediately passing behind left leg to form Cross Stance (S-E). At same time, right hand raises sword right, back and up to perform Binding the Head, blade-edge out, point down. Left palm moves down to left side then forward and pulled in to right chest, fingers up, palm facing out. Gaze forward. (Diag. F.34.2)

Diag. F. 34.1   Diag. F. 34.2

c) Carry straight on. Torso turns 180° to right, left foot crossing behind right (S-E), both legs bending to full squat to form Rest Stance. At same time, right hand brings sword around left shoulder, past front of body, cutting down to lower right, blade-edge slanting down, point forward. Left palm pushes out to upper left, palm facing left, fingers forward. Gaze on sword body. (Diag. F. 34.3)

Diag. F. 34.3

Essentials:

The three movements must be completed successively. Forward Step, Cross Stance and Binding the Head must be completed together. The turn, Cross Stance turning into Rest Stance and Downward Cut must all be completed together. Twist waist to right when performing Downward Cut, right arm pulling sword to right rear.

32. ENTWINING THE HEAD WITH SPRING KICK

a) Legs straighten. Pivoting on the heel of the right foot and ball of the left foot, turn left 270° into Parallel Open Step (facing South). At same time, right hand raises sword past front of body to left, then up to perform Entwining the Head, blade-edge to rear, point down. Left palm is withdrawn to in front of right chest, fingers up, palm facing out. Gaze forward. (Diag. F.35.1)

b) Left foot rises up and shifts a pace forward, toes turned out. Torso turns left (N-E). Right leg stretches straight out forward, foot extended, in Spring Kick (S-E). At same time, right hand swings round to right, forward and left in an arc to Round the Middle Concealing, blade-edge out, point to rear. Left palm is raised up, palm up, fingers right. Gaze forward. (Diag. F. 35. 2)

Diag. F. 35.1   Diag. F. 35.2

Essentials:

Perform the Spring Kick once the Turn and the Round the Middle Concealing have been completed. Kick should be to waist height.

33. COVERING STEP WITH BRANDISH, BOW STANCE WITH SIDE PARRY

a) Right foot lands in front of body (S-E), toes turned out. Torso turns right. Left foot rises and swings straight out to left side. At same time, right hand swings sword

forward and to right to right side of body. Forearm turns
out, straight arm rises up so that sword point swings back
and left, finishing horizontal above head, blade-edge up,
point left. Left palm swings down to left side with straight
arm, palm down. Gaze to lower left. (Diag. F.36.1)

b) Carry straight on. Left foot passes in front of
right leg to outer right in Covering Step (W), toes turned
out, knee slightly bent, right leg straightening to form
Cross Stance. At same time, right hand brings sword left
and down to stop at left side, blade-edge down, point left.
Left palm rests on right wrist. Gaze on sword body.
(Diag. F.36.2)

Diag. F. 36.1   Diag. F. 36.2

c) Carry straight on. Pivoting on heel of left foot and
ball of right, spin body to upper right. At same time,
right hand follows turn swinging sword left, up and to
right, blade-edge down, point right. Left palm follows
turn and extends out to side of body. Gaze forward.
(Diag. F. 36. 3.)

d) Right wrist revolves so that sword performs Wrist
Shearing Flourish outside right forearm, stopping above

head, blade-edge up, point to rear. Torso turns slightly to right and the right knee rises up. Left palm rests on right wrist. Gaze forward. (Diag. F.36.4)

Diag. F. 36.3   Diag. F. 36.4

e) Left heel turns out, torso turning right. Right foot lands to right side (W, N-W), knee bending to half squat, left leg straightening to form Right Bow Stance. At same time, right hand pulls sword level to right side, Parrying in front of chest, arm higher than shoulder, gripping palm down, blade-edge forward, point left. Left palm leaves wrist, turns to Hook and extends out to left side with straight arm, slightly lower than shoulder height, Hook pointing up. Head turns left, gaze forward. (Diag. F. 36. 5)

Essentials:

The five movements should be completed successively. Covering Step and swing of sword to left hip should be completed together. The turn of the waist in c) d) and e) and the right foot landing to right side should be rapid. Bow Stance, Parry and Hook should all be completed together. Torso should tilt to right during Side Parry.

34. TURN WITH ENTWINING THE HEAD, INWARD KICK

a) Left foot takes a step forward (S-W), toes turned in. The toes of right foot turns out. At same time, right hand lifts sword up round left shoulder to perform Entwining the Head, blade-edge out, point down. Left Hook changes to palm and is withdrawn to in front of right chest, fingers up, palm out. Gaze forward. (Diag. F.37.1)

Diag. F. 36.5   Diag. F. 37.1

b) Carry straight on. Toes of left foot turn out, weight shifts forward. At same time, right hand swings sword right, forward and left in an arc to form Round the Middle Concealing, blade-edge out, point to rear. Right leg swings up and in, left palm striking right sole in front of head. Gaze on right foot. (Diag. F. 37. 2)

Essentials:

The two movements must be completed successively. Strike of Inward Kick must be crisp and accurate.

35. LEAPING STEP WITH WAVE

a) Right foot lands in front of left then immediately

Diag. F. 37.2

takes a step to right front (S-W). At same time, right hand swings sword level to front and right, blade-edge to rear, point right. Left palm swings level to left side, palm down. Head turns right, gaze on sword point. (Diag. F. 38.1)

b) Spring into air from right foot, torso turning right (chest facing N-W). Left foot leaps sideways to left side, toes turned in as foot lands (S-W). At same time, following turn of torso during leap right arm raises sword back and up to perform Binding the Head, blade-edge out, point down. Left palm is withdrawn to in front of right chest, fingers up, palm out. Gaze forward. (Diag. F. 38.2)

c) Pivoting on ball of left foot, turn 180° to right, right foot landing to fore (S-W), knee bending to half squat, left leg straightening to form Right Bow Stance. At same time, right hand brings sword round left shoulder, swinging it forward horizontally with straight arm, blade-edge right, point forward. Left palm rests on right wrist. Gaze on sword point. (Diag. F.38.3)

| Diag. F. 38.1 | Diag. F. 38.2 |

Diag. F. 38.3

d) Weight shifts back, left leg bending to half squat, right leg straightening. Torso tilts over to left. At same time, keeping arm straight, wrist revolves so that the sword swings round right to in front of right shoulder, blade-edge up, point right. Left palm rests on inner right forearm. Gaze on sword point. (Diag. F.38.4)

Essentials:

The four movements should be completed successively. The direction of the leaping turn should face S-W, the

Diag. F. 38.4   Diag. F. 39

leap high and far.

The scope of the Wave should be large. When sword is forward, tilt body forward as much as possible and when sword waves in front of right shoulder, torso should be fully tilted to left.

36. KNEE RAISE WITH HORIZONTAL CHOP

Carry straight on. Support body on right foot. Left knee rises in front of body to form Knee Raise Balance. At same time, sword swings left and forward in a reverse wrist Horizontal Chop, gripping palm down, sword and arm in a straight line at shoulder height, blade-edge to rear, point right (S-W). Left palm rises up above head in Exposed Palm, fingers right, palm up. Gaze on sword point. (Diag. F.39)

Essentials:

Left foot should spring off ground with force for Knee Raise so as to help the body straighten up. Knee Raise and Horizontal Chop should be completed together.

37. CROUCHING STANCE WITH UPWARD THRUST

Left foot lands to side (N-E), knee bending to full squat, right leg straightening to form Crouching Stance. At same time, right forearm turns out so blade-edge is down. Wrist sinks so sword thrusts up and sword body hangs erect, blade-edge forward, point up. Gaze on sword point. (Diag. F. 40)

Essentials:

Crouching Stance and Upward Thrust should be completed together.

Right arm must be straight.

38. LEG HOOK WITH JAB

a) Body rises up slightly. At same time, right hand swings sword point forward and down on the inside of right arm in an upright circular Wrist Shearing Flourish, immediately followed by another Wrist Shearing Flourish on the outside of the arm, sword stopping at right side with upright sword, blade-edge forward, point up. Left palm rests on right forearm. Gaze on sword point. (Diag. F.41.1)

Diag. F. 40   Diag. F. 41.1

b) Weight shifts forward, right leg bending to half squat. Left foot, stretched out straight, rises to hook behind right knee. At same time, right arm extends straight out, wrist bending down, sword point jabbing to right, blade-edge down, point to lower right. Left palm rises up above head to form Exposed Palm, fingers right, palm up. Gaze on sword point. (Diag. F.41.2)

Diag. F. 41.2

Essentials:

During the two successive Wrist Shearing Flourishes, the arm must be straight, wrist revolving powerfully, blade following a circular path close in to arm. Leg Hook and Jab should be completed together. Jab should be fast and powerful with wrist relaxed so force reaches point.

Routine III:

39. CROSS STANCE WITH REVERSE SWEEP THRUST

Left foot lands to rear. Right foot then passes behind left to rear (N-E) to form Cross Stance. At same time, right forearm turns out, so blade-edge faces up, straight right arm swinging up and to left, arm then bending and continuing to rear, down and forward in a Reverse Sweep Thrust, thumb down, blade-edge up, point to lower front. Left palm rests on right forearm. Gaze on sword point. (Diag. F. 42)

Diag. F.42

Essentials:

Left foot landing to rear and right arm moving up should be completed together. Cross Stance and Reverse Sweep Thrust should be completed together. Sweep Thrust should keep close to left side, sword path circular.

40. KNEE RAISE WITH CONCEALING, STAB TO ATTENTION

a) Carry straight on. Pivoting on right foot, left knee rises up in front of body and torso turns 180° to right rear (N-E). Following turn of body right hand raises sword up, with straight arm performing a Wrist Shearing Flourish outside the arm above the head. When sword starts to move forward again, right arm follows forward, down and to rear, pulling sword to Concealing position, blade-edge down, point forward. Left palm pushes out forward, palm right, edge of little finger forward. Gaze forward. (Diag. F.43.1)

Diag. F. 43.1

b) Carry straight on. Left foot lands to front left (N-E), then leaping off the ground, right foot leaping forward to land on ground. Left foot quickly moves up to join right foot to attention, both legs bent to half squat. At same time, sword passes waist and stabs to lower front, sword slanting down, blade-edge down, point forward. Left wrist rests on right forearm. Gaze on sword point. (Diag. F.43.2)

Essentials:

The forward leap should be long, Stab and feet coming to attention completed together. The two movements should be completed successively.

41. LEAPING STEP WITH DOWNWARD HACK

a) Legs straighten, right foot taking a step forward to form Front-Back Open Step. At same time, right

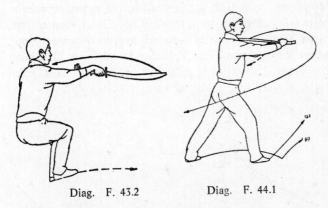

Diag. F. 43.2   Diag. F. 44.1

forearm turns in, arm bends slightly and wrist bends to make sword swing to left, blade-edge out, point to rear. Left palm rests on right wrist. Gaze forward. (Diag. F. 44. 1)

b) Left foot takes a step forward and as soon as it touches the ground it leaps off into the air. Right knee rises up in front of body. At same time, right hand swings sword forward, right and to rear in a Downward Hack, blade-edge to rear, point slanting down. Left palm is withdrawn to in front of right chest, palm down, fingers right, head turns right, gaze on sword point. (Diag. F. 44. 2)

Essentials:

Leap must be long and high, right knee lifted up as high as possible. Waist turns to lower right during Downward Hack. Leap, Downward Hack and movement of palm must all be completed together.

42. ENTWINING THE HEAD WITH SPIN

a) Left foot lands, right foot then landing in front of

left. Once right foot has landed, left foot then immediately takes another step forward (N-E). At same time, right hand raises sword forward and up, blade-edge out, point down, round left shoulder to perform Entwining the Head. Left palm is pulled in in front of chest, palm right, fingers up. Gaze forward. (Diag. F.45.1)

Diag. F. 44.2   Diag. 45.1

b) Right foot takes a step forward (E), chest facing North. At same time, right hand swings sword right and out to right side, arm straight, sword and arm forming a straight line, blade-edge forward, point right. Left palm swings straight out to left side, palm forward, fingers left. Head turns right, gaze on sword point. (Diag. F. 45. 2)

c) Torso turns 180° to left rear. Left foot follows turn, taking a stride to left side (E), ball of foot touching ground. Torso leans forward and twists to left. At same time, sword swings round level following turn. Left palm also swings round level following turn. Head turns left, gaze forward and down. (Diag. F.45.3)

Diag. F. 45.2

Diag. F. 45.3

d) Carry straight on. Weight shifts forward, torso swinging left. Left foot leaps off ground, right leg swinging up behind body, immediately after which left leg also swings to rear and up, both legs in mid-air, chest down, body horizontal. At same time, sword swings round level under body to left for a complete revolution with arm bent. Left arm follows turn of body, swinging out level to left. Stick out chest, raise head, gaze forward. (Diag. F. 45. 4)

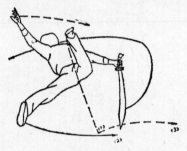

Diag. F. 45.4

Essentials:

The steps forward must be quick and powerful as a proper preparation for the completion of the spin in mid-air. If for the time being one cannot complete the spin, then one can change it to a Turn with Entwining the Head.

43. LEFT SWIPE

a) Carry straight on. Right foot lands first, left foot landing behind right (E), right foot then taking another step backward, leg extending to form Left Bow Stance. At same time, right hand swipes forward, blade-edge forward, point right. Left palm swings out level to left, palm forward, fingers left. Head turns right, gaze on sword point. (Diag. F.46)

Essentials:

The two retreating steps after landing should be quick. Swipe should swing out in an arc. Once Bow Stance is completed, Swipe finishes.

Diag. F. 46

44. BOW STANCE WITH DOWNWARD STAB

a) Carry straight on. Weight shifts back, left foot slides back a step (E), heel raised. At same time, right hand swings sword in an arc slightly to left, then pulling it back to right rear to Concealing position, blade-edge down, point forward. Left palm thrusts forward past waist in Palm Push, fingers up, palm forward. Gaze forward. (Diag. F.47.1)

b) Carry straight on. Right foot slides back a step (N-E), leg straightens, left leg bending to half squat to

Diag. F. 47.1

form Left Bow Stance.   At same time, right hand thrusts sword past waist to lower front in a Stab, blade-edge down, point to lower front. Left palm swings down past waist and up again to left rear, palm forward, fingers left.   Gaze on sword point. (Diag. F. 47.2)

Essentials:

Movements must be continuous. Feet sliding back must be quite slow and smooth. During sliding step body should not bob up and down or sway, legs remaining bent and the right leg springing straight for the final Bow Stance. Bow Stance and Stab must be coordinated.

45. TURN TO BOW STANCE WITH DOWNWARD STAB

a) Left foot springs off ground, knee rising up, right leg supporting body. At same time, wrist turns up with straight right arm so sword comes up and back with back resting on right shoulder, blade-edge up, point to rear. Left palm rests on right wrist. Gaze on blade-edge. (Diag. F.48.1)

b) Carry straight on.   Pivoting on ball of right foot,

Diag. F. 47.2   Diag. F. 48.1

turn torso 270° to right rear (chest facing S), torso leaning forward slightly. During turn right hand does not move, but once turn is finished, bend hand up in front of chest so that elbow touches sword body, the hilt high, the point low, blade-edge forward, point to lower front. Left palm rests on right wrist, elbow pointing up. Gaze on sword point. (Diag. F. 48. 2)

c) Left foot lands to left front (S-W) to form Left Bow Stance. A same time, right arm stabs sword straight to lower front (W), blade-edge down, point forward. Left palm thrusts out to left rear, palm left, fingers to rear. Gaze on sword point. (Diag. F. 48.3)

Diag. F. 48.2   Diag. F. 48.3

Essentials:

The three movements must be completed successively. The turn must be quick and well balanced.

46. TURN WITH DOWNWARD VERTICAL SLASH, BOW STANCE WITH CONCEALING

a) Left leg straightens, toes turn in. Torso turns to right (E). Right foot leaves ground and takes a stride out to right (S-E). At same time, right hand swings sword left so sword-back sticks close in to left ribs in a Round the Middle Concealing, blade-edge left, point to rear. Left palm rises up above head, palm up, fingers to right. Gaze forward. (Diag. F. 49. 1)

b) Carry straight on. Pivoting on ball of right foot, torso turns to right rear for a full revolution. Left foot follows turn and lands a step forward (E) beside right foot (about a foot's distance between them). At same time, right hand raises sword forward, right and back to perform Binding the Head, then round left shoulder, arm dropping down so sword is by left leg, blade-edge out, point down. Left palm moves down to rest on right wrist. Gaze on sword body. (Diag. F.49.2)

Diag. F. 49.1　　　　Diag. F. 49.2

c) Carry straight on. Weight shifts forward. Right knee rises up. Pivoting on left foot, turn body to right rear for one and a half turns. At same time, sword remains in same position, following turn of body, arms extended in a Vertical Slash, finishing facing west. Gaze on sword-body. (Diag. F.49.3)

d) Right foot lands to right front (N-W), knee bending to half squat, left leg straightening to form Right Bow Stance. At same time, right hand pulls sword right and back to form concealing, blade-edge down, point forward. Left palm pushes out to front, edge of little finger forward, fingers up. Gaze forward. (Diag. F.49.4)

Diag. F. 49.3   Diag. F. 49.4

Essentials:
The four movements must be continuous. Arms must be straight during Vertical Slash, sword hanging erect, blade-edge facing direction of turn. Turn should pivot on ball of left foot, leg straight, the turn fast and stable. Bow Stance, Concealing and Palm Push must be completed together.

47. COVERING STEP WITH BRANDISH, LEAPING TURN WITH WRIST FLOURISH, BOW STANCE WITH STAB

a) Toes of right foot turn in, torso turning left (S-E). Left foot rises up, toes turned out, foot landing in front of body. At same time, right hand follows turn and raises sword up to right side, arm straight, blade-edge to rear, point down. Left palm swings out level to left, palm forward, fingers up. Gaze forward. (Diag. F.50.1)

b) Pivoting on ball of left foot, turn torso to left rear (N). Weight shifts to left leg, right foot leaves ground and following turn swings out to right side (E). At same time, right hand swings sword forward, left and up to a horizontal parry above head, blade-edge up, point left. Left palm is withdrawn in front of right chest. Gaze forward. (Diag. F.50.2)

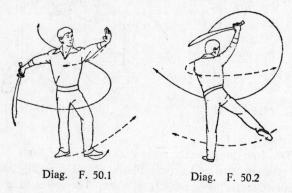

Diag. F. 50.1   Diag. F. 50.2

c) Carry sraight on. Torso turns left (S). Right foot follows turn and lands in front of body (W), knee bends to half squat, left leg straightens to form Right Bow Stance. At same time, right hand swings sword back, down and forward in a Sweep Thrust, blade-edge up, point forward. Left palm swings down and up level with shoulder. Gaze on sword point. (Diag. F.50.3)

d) Torso turns to left rear (chest facing E), weight shifting to left leg, knee bent. Toes of right foot turn in. At same time, right hand swings sword up, turning right forearm in as one does so, so blade-edge faces up, point slanting up. Left palm swings down and to rear,

Diag. 50.3

Diag. F. 50.4

palm down. Gaze forward. (Diag. F.50.4)

e) Left foot leaps into air, right foot leaps forward (E), torso turning 180° to left rear (W) in mid-air. Right foot lands with toes turned in (W), left foot raised up behind right. At same time, during leap right hand performs Upright Wrist Shearing Flourish inside forearm with arm straight. After turn right arm is extended behind body, sword point up, blade-edge to rear. Left palm rests by left hip. Gaze forward. (Diag. F.50.5)

Diag. F. 50.5

f) Left foot lands behind right (E), leg straightens, right leg bends at knee to form Right Bow Stance. At same time, right wrist bends down, so that sword passes right hip and forward in straight Stab, shoulder and arm in straight line at shoulder height, blade-edge down, point forward. Left palm swings out level to rear, palm forward, fingers left. Gaze on sword point. (Diag. F.50.6)

Essentials:

The six movements must be completed successively. The Brandishes and Flourish must be continuous, their paths circular and strength flowing in same direction. Wrist Flourish is completed before turn in mid-air is at highest point of leap. Bow Stance and Stab must be completed together.

48. BACK REST WITH ARC STEPS

a) Weight shifts to slightly bent left leg, right knee rising up in front of body. Torso turning slightly to right (chest facing S). At same time, right hand raises sword up and to left, then wrist bends so that sword sticks close

Diag. F. 50.6

down inside of right arm, blade-edge forward, point down. Left palm changes to hook and swings to rear, hook point up. Head turns left, gaze forward. (S-E). (Diag. F.51.1)

b) The four arc steps:

Right toes turn out and foot lands to right front (toes facing W). Torso turns slightly to right. Right arm moves down and bends slightly so that sword is horizontal across chest at shoulder height, blade-edge out, point left. Head turns left, gaze backward. (Diag. F.51.2)

Torso does not move. Toes of left foot turn in, foot

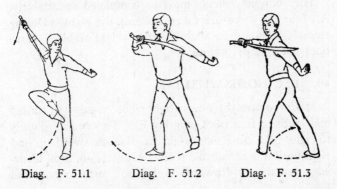

Diag. F. 51.1   Diag. F. 51.2   Diag. F. 51.3

landing in front of and to right of right foot (toes facing N-W). (Diag. F.51.3)

Torso does not move. Toes of right foot turn out, foot passing left instep and landing to right front (toes pointing N-E). (Diag. F.51.4)

Torso does not move. Toes of left foot turn in, foot landing in front of right foot (toes pointing E). (Diag. F.51.5)

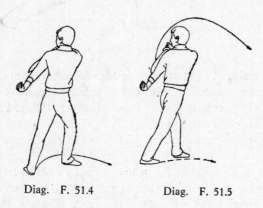

Diag. F. 51.4   Diag. F. 51.5

Essentials:

The four movements must be completed successively. All four arc steps are taken towards the right. During steps legs should be slightly bent, weight stable. Torso does not change posture.

49. LEG HOOK WITH JAB

a) Carry straight on. Right foot passes left instep and lands to fore (toes pointing E). Torso turns slightly to right. At same time, right hand raises sword up and right until it is extended out level with straight arm, blade-edge down, point forward. Left Hook turns to palm and swings out to left side, palm forward, fingers left. (Diag. F.52.1)

b) Right leg bends to half squat, left foot rises and hooks in behind right knee. At same time, right hand performs an upright Wrist Shearing Flourish outside right arm, wrist then bending down so that force reaches sword point, jabbing forward (E), hilt higher than right shoulder. Left palm moves forward to rest on right inner fore arm. Gaze on point. (Diag. F.52.2)

Diag. F. 52.1   Diag. F. 52.2

Essentials:
Leg Hook and Jab should continue on from the arc steps. Jab and complete Leg Hook together after the Wrist Shearing Flourish.

50. WHIRLWIND KICK, SPLITS WITH UPWARD STAB (OR BOW STANCE WITH STAB)

a) Left foot lands to left side of body (N-W). Torso turns left. At same time, right hand swings sword up, left, down and to lower right in a straight arm brandish until it reaches right side, arm raised level,

273

blade-edge to rear, point down. When sword has swung in front of body, left palm pushes out to left side, palm forward, fingers up. Gaze on left palm. (Diag. F.53.1)

b) Carry straight on. Left foot turns out. Toes of right foot turn in, then right foot immediately takes a step forwards (N-W), ball of foot touching ground, leg slightly bent (in preparation for springing off ground). At same time, right hand swings sword up, forward and down to front of body, blade-edge out, point down. Left palm rests on right inner forearm. Gaze to lower front. (Diag. F.53.2)

Diag. F. 53.1   Diag. F. 53.2

c) Carry straight on. Right foot springs off ground, body spinning round and up to left rear. Left leg leaves ground, knee raised up in front of body. Right leg swiftly executes an Inward Kick, sole of foot turned in. When body has turned 270° left palm strikes right foot. In mid-air right hand swings sword level round to left waist. Gaze on right foot. (Diag. F.53.3)

d) Once Whirlwind Kick is completed, both feet land in Splits, left leg to fore (S-E), right leg to rear (N-W). Torso leans forward. Right hand thrusts sword to upper

Diag. F. 53.4

fore in a Stab, blade-edge down, point to front upper right (S-E). At same time, left palm thrusts out to left rear, palm left, fingers to rear. Gaze on sword-point. (Diag. F.53.4)

Note: If one cannot execute the Splits, then change it to a Left Bow Stance. Thus, when Whirlwind Kick is finished, left foot lands first, right leg stretching out to rear to form Bow Stance. Directions all the same. Torso the same. (Diag. F.53.5)

Essentials:

The four movements must be completed successively.
The Whirlwind Kick in mid-air must be high and fast,
the slap crisp and accurate.

51. RISE FROM SPLITS TO UPWARD PARRY

Head and torso straighten up, legs withdrawn at same
time so that knees come together at half squat, balls of
feet touching ground, torso turning right (W). At same
time, right hand parries up with straight arm, blade-edge
up, point left. Left palm swings round to front, fingers
up. Gaze forward. (Diag. F.54)

Diag. F. 53.5   Diag. F. 54

Essentials:

Rise from splits, torso turning right and Upward Parry
must all be completed together. If one performs Bow
Stance with Stab, one should withdraw left foot to beside right. At same time, turn torso right and Parry upward.

Routine IV:

52. WAVE WITH BINDING THE HEAD

a) Both legs straighten up. Pivoting on the ball of the left foot, turn to left rear, right foot taking a step forward (E). At same time, right forearm turns out, so sword waves above head from left to right, blade-edge up, point to upper rear. Left palm rests on right wrist. Lean head and torso back. Gaze on sword body. (Diag. F.55.1)

b) Torso turns left (N-E), left foot takes a step forward (N-E), toes turning in to form Front-back Open Stance. At same time, right hand swings sword right, forward and to left close in to ribs to form Round the Middle Concealing, blade-edge out, point to rear. Left palm rises up, palm up, fingers right. Gaze forward. (Diag. F.55.2)

Diag. F. 55.1   Diag. F. 55.2

c) Pivoting on ball of left foot, immediately turn to right rear (N-W). Right foot then takes a step out to right (N-E) to form Parallel Open Stance. At same time, right hand raises sword forward, right and up to perform Binding the Head, blade-edge to rear, point down. Left palm is withdrawn to in front of right chest. Gaze forward. (Diag. F.55.3)

Diag. F. 55.3   Diag. F. 56.1

Essentials:

The three movements must be completed successively, without halting in middle. When Wave reaches front of body one should raise head and tilt body back. Wave should be slightly higher than body. Open Stance and Round the Middle Concealing, Side Step and Binding the Head should all be well coordinated.

53. TURN WITH BRANDISH OF ARMS, KNEE RAISE WITH STAB

a) Carry straight on. Torso turns slightly to right (N). Right leg bends, left foot is withdrawn to right instep, toes touching ground. At same time, right hand brings sword around left shoulder to front of body and down, then from right side up. When sword and arm extend straight up, bend wrist so sword is horizontal above head, blade-edge up, point left. Left palm pushes out to left, fingers up, edge of little finger forward. Head turns left, gaze forward. (Diag. F.56.1)

b) Carry straight on. Torso turns left (S), left foot taking a step forward (W), toes turned out. Straight right leg swings out and round following turn, foot stretched straight. Right forearm turns out, and following turn, right hand brandishes sword left, down and up, until it is raised slanting down above head, blade-edge left, point down. Left arm bends down, palm then withdrawn to right chest. Gaze on sword point. (Diag. F.56.2)

Diag. F. 56.2   Diag. F. 56.3

c) Right foot lands in front of left (E) in Open Stance. Torso turns left (E). At same time, right hand brings sword right and down, wrist bending so that sword body is brought in close to waist to form Concealing, blade-edge down, point forward. Left palm swings down, left and up to form Upright Palm in front of body, palm right, edge of little finger forward, fingers up. Gaze on left palm. (Diag. F.56.3)

d) Right leg supports whole body, left knee raises in front of body to form Knee Raise Balance. At same time, right hand thrusts sword out past waist in a Stab (E), sword and arm in a straight line at shoulder height, blade-edge down, point forward. Left palm rests on right arm. Gaze on sword point. (Diag. F.56.4)

Diag. F. 56.4

Essentials:
The four movements must be completed successively. The Brandish during the turn must be circular and stick close to the body. Knee Raise and Stab must be completed together.

54. AIDING RUN WITH SIDEWAYS MID-AIR SPIN

a) Torso turns left, left foot landing to left(W). At same time, right forearm turns in and wrist bends so sword point follows turn to lower front to form Concealing, blade-edge slanting to rear, point slanting down. Left palm pushes out to left. Gaze forward. (Diag. F.57.1)

b) Carry straight on. Run forward three steps, end-

Diag. F. 57.1

ing with right foot to front. Following steps right hand
swings sword back and to right. Left arm remains out
to left. Gaze forward. (Diag. F.57.2)

Diag. F. 57.2

c) Carry straight on. Torso leans forward. Right foot
hops a step forward. Left knee rises and left foot immediately lands to front. Right foot swings back and up.
Right hand swings sword forward to right side. Left
hand swings naturally down to left side. (Diag. F.57.3)

Diag. F. 57.3

d) Carry straight on. Left foot springs off ground.
Torso tilts forward. Both legs swing forward in mid-air
to form Side Spin. At same time, right hand swings
sword to left then to right underneath body. (Diag.
F.57.4)

e) Feet land, right foot forward(E), left foot to rear,
torso facing East. Right hand finishes swing of sword
under body, stopping at right side, blade-edge slanting
to lower rear, point slanting to lower front. Gaze to
lower front. (Diag. F.57.5)

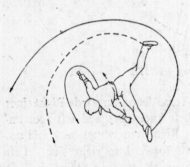

Diag. F. 57.4

Diag. F. 57.5

f) Carry straight on. Feet do not move. Torso turns left (N). Right hand swings sword left to Round the Middle Concealing. Left Palm swings up above head, palm up, fingers right. Gaze forward. (Diag. F.57.6)

Essentials:

The six movements must be completed successively. The aiding run must be quick, the spring off powerful. Swing of sword underneath body must be well coordinated with mid-air Spin. If one cannot complete the mid-air Spin one can do it with the aid of the left hand touching the ground and supporting the body.

55. REST STANCE WITH CONCEALING

a) Torso turns to right rear. Left toes turn in, right foot takes a Reverse Step to rear (W) to form Parallel Open Stance. At same time, right hand raises sword forward, right and up to perform Binding the Head, blade-edge to rear, point down. Left palm withdraws to right chest. Gaze forward. (Diag. F.58.1)

b) Carry straight on. Left foot takes a step behind right (N-W), ball of foot touching ground, legs crossed

Diag. F. 57.6   Diag. F. 58.1

and knees bent to full squat to form Rest Stance. At same time, right hand brings sword round left shoulder, past front of body to right, down and to rear to form Concealing, blade-edge down, point forward. Left palm pushes out to front, edge of little finger to fore, fingers up. Gaze forward past left palm. (Diag. F.58.2)

Diag. F. 58.2

Essentials:
The two movements must be completed successively. The turn and Reverse Step and the Binding the Head must be well coordinated. Rest Stance, Concealing and Palm Push must be completed together.

56. BRANDISHING SLICE, KNEE RAISE WITH STAB

a) Legs straighten up, left foot takes a step forward (E). At same time, right hand swings sword back, up and forward in a Slice, blade-edge down, point forward. Left palm rests on right upper arm. Gaze on sword point. (Diag. F.59.1)

b) Carry straight on. Torso turns left (N). Right foot follows swinging forward and out to right side, leg straight, foot extended. At same time, right hand brings sword down, left and up above head in a slanting Parry, blade-edge slanting up, point slanting down. Left palm is withdrawn in front of chest, palm right, fingers up. Head turns right, gaze forward. (Diag. F.59.2)

Diag. F. 59.1   Diag. F. 59.2

c) Carry straight on. Right foot lands to fore (W). Torso turns left (S-W). Right leg supports body, left knee rises up in front of body to form Knee Raise Balance. At same time, right hand swings sword right and down, then thrusts out forward past waist in a level Stab with arm straight (W), sword and arm in a straight line at shoulder height, blade-edge down, point right. Left palm moves forward and rests on right upper arm. Gaze on sword point. (Diag. F.59.3)

Essentials:

The three movements must be completed successively. Arm must be straight during Brandish, the path of the sword circular. Stab and Knee Raise Balance should be completed together.

Diag. F. 59.3

57. BOW STANCE WITH CONCEALING

Torso turns left. Left foot lands to fore (E), knee bending to half squat, right leg straightening to form Left Bow Stance. At same time, right forearm turns in, wrist bending down so sword point drops to lower front to form Concealing, blade-edge slanting to rear, point slanting down. Left palm follows turn and pushes out to front, fingers up, edge of little finger forward. Gaze in direction of left hand. (Diag. F.60)

Essentials:

The turn should be quick. Bow Stance, Concealing and Palm Push should all be completed together.

58. RECEIVING SWORD

a) Weight shifts to rear, left leg slightly bent. At same time, right hand brings sword forward and up to form Upright Sword, blade-edge forward, point up. Left arm bends slightly, left palm pressing on right wrist. Gaze on left palm. (Diag. F.61.1)

b) Right hand relaxes and slips down sword hilt slightly. Left palm turns up, "Tiger's Mouth" forward,

| Diag. F. 60 | Diag. F. 61.1 |

then slots onto hilt below guard and above right "Tiger's Mouth." All four fingers except thumb grip sword guard. Right hand relaxes grip of hilt, palm turns down and rests on left forearm. Gaze on hilt. (Diag. F. 61.2)

Essentials:

When exchanging sword there can be a gap between the left and right hands on the hilt. When Receiving Sword, left hand must hook hold of guard so that the sword point remains facing up.

59. EMPTY STANCE WITH UPRIGHT SWORD

Carry straight on. Torso turns slightly to right, weight shifts back. Right leg bends to half squat. Left foot shifts a little to rear, toes touching ground to form Left Empty Stance. At same time, left forearm turns in so sword spins right, down, left and up in a circle, ending in reverse grip, sword upright outside left arm, blade-edge forward, point up. Right palm swings down, left, up and forward and rests back on inner arm, palm slanting down, fingers up. Gaze forward. (Diag. F.62)

Essentials:

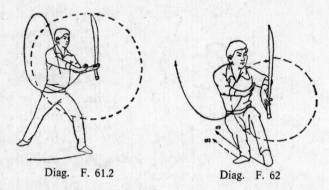

Diag. F. 61.2   Diag. F. 62

Left Empty Stance and right palm resting on inner arm must be completed together. Arms should circle outward.

60. EMBRACING WITH EXPOSED PALM

Left foot takes a step to rear and right foot immediately draws up beside left to attention, both legs straight, toes facing Southwest, chest facing the same direction. At same time, left forearm turns out so sword spins left, down, right, and up in a circle, point up, blade-edge forward, sword now embraced inside left arm, sword back resting against upper arm. Right palm swings down and right to side of body at shoulder height, forearm turning in, wrist bending to form Exposed Palm, palm out (N-W), fingers forward. Head turns left, gaze forward. (Diag. F.63)

Essentials:

Sword spin, legs straightening and Right Exposed Palm should all be well coordinated. Pull right shoulder back, stick left chest forward, attention full, gaze far into distance.

288

Closing Postures, Returning to the Starting Postures

Left foot takes a step forward (S), right foot comes up beside left. Left arm embraces sword and right arm relaxes, both arms hanging naturally by sides. Head turns right, Gaze forward. (Diag. F.64)

Diag. F. 63   Diag. F. 64

Diagram of Foot Positions and Rules for Advanced Routine

To aid the practitioner's practice from the diagrams, the accurate grasping of the requirements of the routine and the understanding of the continuity of the routine, the foot positions of the routine from start to finish are mapped out for reference. (See diagram)

In general, the routine starts in the right half of the competition area (any part will do), and must also finish back in the right half. If one forgets a movement or makes a mistake and finishes in the left half of the area, then one will be penalized. If one's routine must finish in the left half, then one must inform the judges in advance, otherwise one will be penalized.

The positions in the diagram are not absolute, since, of course, each person's size and range of movement are different. However, direction of movement must be strictly adhered to. Apart from being accurate and crisp, the movements must be spread out across the whole performance area, not all cramped together in one part. Practitioners can work out their own fixed path for the routine within the area according to the scale of their completed movements.

The competition area is 14 m. long and 8 m. wide, cut in half by a line down the middle.

If, during competition, a part of the body extends over the limit of the competition area then one has 0.1 deducted (from a total of 10 points). If the whole body extends over the boundary, 0.2 is deducted. Thus it is imperative to keep within the limits of the competition area.

North (rear)
Northwest (right rear)
North by West
North by East
Northeast (left rear)
West by North
East by North
East (left)
West by South
East by South
Southwest (right front)
South by West
South (front)
South by East
Southeast (left front)

Section 4

SINGLE BROADSWORD DUAL ROUTINES

Dual Routine I:

1) A ... Embracing to Attention
   B ... Embracing to Attention
2) A ... Embracing with Exposed Palm
   B ... Embracing with Exposed Palm
3) A ... Embracing with Palm Push
   B ... Embracing with Palm Push
4) A ... Sword Exchange to Attention
   B ... Sword Exchange to Attention
5) A ... Bow Stance with Sweep Thrust
   B ... Bow Stance with Sweep Thrust
6) A ... T-Stance with Embracing
   B ... T-Stance with Embracing
7) A ... Advancing Step with Binding the Head
   B ... Retreating Step with Binding the Head
8) A ... T-Stance with Concealing
   B ... T-Stance with Concealing
9) A ... Step Forward with Slice
   B ... Side Bow Stance with Slice to Wrist
10) A ... T-Stance with Parry and Hand Contact
    B ... T-Stance with Parry and Hand Contact
11) A ... Jump With Hack
    B ... Crouching Stance with Sweep
12) A ... Knee Raise with Cut to Wrist
    B ... Bow Stance with Hack to Leg
13) A ... Falling Step with Level Swipe
    B ... Open Stance with Upright Sword

14) A ... Bow Stance with Downward Hack
    B ... Knee Raise with Cut to Wrist
15) A ... Step Forward with Sword Push
    B ... Step Forward and Lean Back
16) A ... Rest Stance Turning Body to Hack at Leg
    B ... Cross Stance Turning Body to Cut at Wrist
17) A ... Turn with Entwining the Head
    B ... Turn, Step Forward and Chop
18) A ... Kneel with Sweep
    B ... Knee Raise with Embracing
19) A ... Knee Raise with Chop
    B ... Kneel with Sweep
20) A ... Cross Stance with Concealing
    B ... Cross Stance with Concealing
21) A ... Horse Stance with Stab
    B ... Horse Stance with Stab
22) A ... Step Forward with Sweep Thrust
    B ... Step Forward with Sweep Thrust
23) A ... Cross Stance with Concealing
    B ... Cross Stance with Concealing
24) A ... Bow Stance with Stab
    B ... Twist with Vertical Slash
25) A ... Forward Leap to Rest Stance with Downward Cut
    B ... Turning Leap to Bow Stance with Stab
26) A ... Advancing Step with Sweep Thrust
    B ... Kneel and Parry
27) A ... Step Forward with Downward Stab
    B ... Knee Raise with Left Side Press
28) A ... T-Stance with Withdrawl of Sword
    B ... Falling Step with Raised Sword
29) A ... Bow Stance with Stab
    B ... Right Side Press

30)	A...	Covering Step with Downward Hack
	B...	Turn to Covering Step and Vertical Slash
31)	A...	T-Stance with Parry
	B...	Backward Cross Stance with Parry
32)	A...	Retreating Step with Sweep Thrust
	B...	Step Forward with Sweep Thrust
33)	A...	Retreating Step with Sweep Thrust
	B...	Step Forward with Sweep Thrust
34)	A...	Turning Leap to Bow Stance with Downward Stab
	B...	Leap to Rest Stance with Downward Cut
35)	A...	Kneel and Parry
	B...	Step Forward with Sweep Thrust
36)	A...	Kneel and Sweep
	B...	Leap with Level Chop
37)	A...	Mid-air Backward Slice
	B...	Bow Stance with Stab
38)	A...	Horse Stance with Downward Cut
	B...	Horse Stance with Downward Sweep Thrust
39)	A...	Cross Stance with Upward Parry
	B...	Step Forward to Brandishing Slice
40)	A...	Left Upward Kick
	B...	Loss of Sword
41)	A...	Land with Embracing
	B...	Step Forward with Side Spring Kick
42)	A...	Back Drop
	B...	Right Outward Swing Kick
43)	A...	Turn to Bow Stance with Concealing
	B...	Palm Push to Attention

Dual Routine I:

The black-haired one is A, the white-haired one B.

1) A ... Embracing to Attention
** B ... Embracing to Attention**

A faces South, B faces North, the two about four paces apart. Both embrace sword in left hand, right hand forming palm, both arms hanging by sides, elbows slightly bent, shoulders pulled back. Heads turned slightly to left, gaze forward. (Diag. G.1)

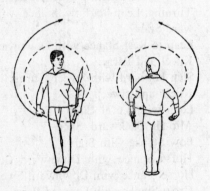

Diag. G. 1

Essentials:

Legs straight, chest out, back erect, conforming to the demands for the Embracing position.

2) A ... Embracing with Exposed Palm
** B ... Embracing with Exposed Palm**

A turns torso slightly to right. Left arm embracing sword swings in a circle from left side, past the abdomen to the right, up, left and down to beside the waist, blade-edge forward, point up. Right palm swings up above head to form Exposed Palm, palm up, fingers facing left. Torso turns slightly to left, head following the same direction. Gaze on opponent.

294

Diag. G. 2

B does the same as A. (Diag. G.2)

Essentials:

The swing of the embraced sword must be powerful and circular. The swing up of right palm should be just after the swing of left arm.

3) A... Embracing with Palm Push
B... Embracing with Palm Push

A turns left 90° (to face East), left foot takes a step forward. Right foot follows up behind left foot to form Attention Stance. A now faces Opponent B. Left arm does not move. Right palm swings in an arc right and down, striking out past waist in a Palm Push (E), fingers up. Gaze on opponent.

B turns 90° to left (to face West). Left foot takes a step forward. Thereafter same as A. (Diag. G.3)

Essentials:

Swing right palm first, then when it reaches waist, turn body left 90°. Palm Push and Attention Posture should be completed together.

4) A... Sword Exchange to Attention
B... Sword Exchange to Attention

Diag. G. 3

A raises left arm up in front of body at shoulder height, blade-edge up, point to rear. Right palm rests on hilt, ready to grasp sword. At same time, both knees bend to half squat, right foot takes a step back (W), right leg straightening to form Left Bow Stance. Gaze on opponent.

B does the same as A, except that his foot takes a step backward to East, torso facing West. (Diag. G.4)

Essentials:

Raising of left arm, right hand moving up to rest on

Diag. G. 4

hilt and step back to form Left Bow Stance should all be completed together.

5) A ... Bow Stance with Sweep Thrust
B ... Bow Stance with Sweep Thrust

A takes a step back with left foot (W), leg straightening. Right leg bends to half squat to form Right Bow Stance. At same time, right hand grasps hilt, straight arm rising up, swinging past right side to rear, down and forward in a Sweep Thrust, blade-edge up, point forward. Right hand releases hilt and turns to palm, then coordinates with movement of sword to swing up and back in an arc with straight arm to left side of body, palm facing forward, fingers left. Gaze on opponent.

B's left foot takes a step back(E), leg straightening. Thereafter the same as A. (Diag. G.5)

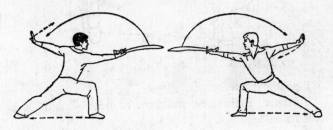

Diag. G. 5

Essentials:

As the sword swings back, torso turns right; as it swings forward, torso turns left. Right Bow Stance, Sweep Thrust and swing of left palm should all be completed together.

6) A ... T-Stance with Embracing
B ... T-Stance with Embracing

A shifts weight back, left leg bending to half squat,

right foot brought in to beside left instep, toes touching ground to form T-Stance (chest facing North). At same time, right hand swings sword up and to left so sword comes over to rest flat on left arm, blade-edge facing out, point to rear. Left arm bends in at elbow so palm rests on right wrist. Head turns right, gaze on opponent.

B's movements are the same as A, except that after the T-Stance, B faces South. (Diag. G.6)

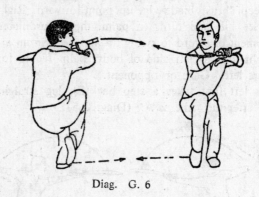

Diag. G. 6

Essentials:

T-Stance, Embracing and turn of head should all be completed together.

7) A... Advancing Step with Binding the Head
    B... Retreating Step with Binding the Head

a) A takes a big step right (E) with right foot, toes pointing East. At same time, right hand follows step and swings out to right in front of body.

B takes a big step right (W) with right foot. Thereafter, the same as A. (Diag. G.7.1)

b) A takes a step forward (S-E) with left foot, legs apart to form Parallel Open Stance. At same time, right hand swings sword level to right side at shoulder height,

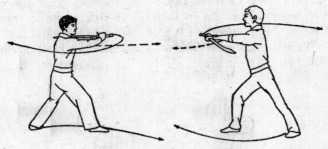

Diag. G. 7.1

blade-edge to rear, point right. Left arm swings straight out to left side, palm down, fingers left. Head turns right, gaze on sword-point.

B takes a step forward (N-W) with left foot. Thereafter, the same as A. (Diag. G.7.2)

Diag. G. 7.2

c) A supports weight on left foot, and, pivoting on the ball of the foot, turns torso round to right rear. Right knee is raised up in front of body, chest facing North. At same time, right arm raises sword back and up, sword-back sticking close to back, blade-edge to rear, point down. Left palm is brought in in front of right chest to form Upright Palm. Gaze on B.

B's movements are same as A, except chest faces South. (Diag. G.7.3)

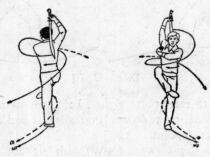

Diag. G. 7.3

Essentials:

All three movements should be continuous.

8) A ... T-Stance with Concealing

B ... T-Stance with Concealing

A carries straight on, torso continuing turn to right rear. Right foot follows turn and lands to right side(S-W). Left foot draws up beside right instep, both legs bending to half squat to form T-Stance. At same time, right hand brings sword round left shoulder, past front of body to right and back to form Concealing position, blade-edge down, point forward. Left palm pushes out from in front of chest, fingers up. Head turns left, gaze on B.

B's movements are same as A, except that he faces N-E. (Diag. G.8)

Essentials:

T-Stance, Palm Push, Concealing, turn and gaze on op-

Diag. G. 8

ponent must all be completed together. Both practitioners'
movements must be simultaneous.

9) A ... Step Forward with Slice
**   B ... Side Bow Stance with Slice to Wrist**

a) A takes a step forward (N-E) with left foot, toes
turned out, knee slightly bent, right leg straight. At same
time, right hand swings sword out to right side, sword
and arm forming a straight line, blade-edge forward, point
right. Left palm presses forward with "Tiger's Mouth"
open. Gaze on B.

B takes a step to front left (S-W) with left foot, toes
turning out, leg slightly bent, right leg straight. At same
time, right hand maintains same Concealing position, not
moving. Left palm presses forward, "Tiger's Mouth"
spread open. Gaze on A. (Diag. G.9.1)

b) A takes a step forward (N-E) with right foot, knee
bending to half squat, left leg straightening to form Right
Bow Stance. At same time, right hand brings sword up
and forward in a Slice to B's head. Left palm swings
down and back in an arc to left side, palm facing left,
fingers up. Gaze on sword-point.

B sees A slicing to head, and takes a step to front
right (W) with right foot, knee bending to half squat, left
leg straightening to form Right Side Bow Stance, thus

Diag. G. 9.1

dodging A's Slice. At same time, right hand swings sword up and forward in a Slice to A's right wrist. Left palm rests on right wrist. Gaze on opponent's wrist. (Diag. G.9.2)

Essentials:

A's Slice to B's head must be accurate, not shifting

Diag. G. 9.2

when he sees B dodge. When B sees A slicing at his head, he must wait until the sword has nearly struck before dodging and slicing at A's wrist.

10)　A . . .　T-Stance with Parry and Hand Contact
　　　B . . .　T-Stance with Parry and Hand Contact

A shifts right foot slightly to right rear, toes turning out. Left foot is then swiftly brought in to beside right instep, both legs bending to half squat to form T-Stance. At same time, straight right arm swings up and right, so sword forms a horizontal Parry above head, blade-edge up, point facing left. Left hand thrusts out to form Upright Palm, wrist connecting with B's wrist. Gaze on opponent.

B turns right foot out, knee bending to half squat, left foot then brought in to beside right instep to form T-Stance. At same time, straight right arm swings up and right so that sword forms a horizontal Parry above head, blade-edge up, point facing left. Left palm thrusts out to form Upright Palm, wrist connecting with A's wrist. Gaze on opponent. (Diag. G.10)

Diag.　G. 10

Essentials:

Both sides must change to T-Stance with Parry once the attack and defence have been clearly completed. Both sides must move simultaneously, wrists firmly, connecting. A is to S-W, B to N-E.

11) A . . . Jump with Hack

   B . . . Crouching Stance with Sweep

(Please note: if B moves first, then B is written first and A after, as below)

B leans forward, left foot taking a large step to left(S), right leg bending to full squat, to form Crouching Stance. At same time, right hand first swings sword down to lower right, then forward at A's legs(S), blade-edge forward. Left palm swings out level to left side. Gaze on sweeping blade.

When A sees B sweeping at legs, he jumps off ground with both feet, leaping over B's blade. At same time, right hand sweeps sword to front right in a Hack at B's head. Left palm swings level out to left side. Gaze on B's head. (Diag. G.11)

Diag. G. 11

Essentials:

Both sides must move simultaneously. B's sweeping blade must be close to the ground, A's Hack not too high.

12) A ... Knee Raise with Cut to Wrist
      B ... Bow Stance with Hack to Leg

B straightens left leg. Right foot takes a step forward(W), knee bending to half squat, left leg straightening to form Right Bow Stance. At same time, right forearm turns inward so blade-edge faces right, then hacking at A's legs. Left palm swings forward to rest on right wrist. Torso leans forward slightly. Gaze on A's legs.

A lands on ground, torso turns slightly to right, right knee rising up. At same time, right forearm turns inward, wrist twisting from right to left, so sword moves up, left and down, using the blade-edge to cut at B's wrist. Left palm is raised up to left side. Gaze on B's wrist. (Diag. G.12)

Essentials:

Both sides must move simultaneously. A is to West, B to East.

Diag. G. 12

13) A ... Falling Step with Level Swipe
B ... Open Stance with Upright Sword

a) A turns torso slightly to right, right foot landing in front of body(E), toes turned out. Left foot passes round right leg, landing in front of body(S), toes turned in. At same time, right hand brings sword right, back and up to perform Binding the Head. When sword has passed round left shoulder, it is held horizontal across left side of body, blade-edge forward, point left. Left arm bends, left hand resting on right wrist. Gaze on B.

B raises right foot, toes turn out, then foot re-alights at original place. Left foot swings round in front of right leg(N), and lands with toes turned in. At same time, right forearm turns out so blade-edge faces up, sword swinging in an arc up, left, back and down to left side of body (S-W). Left hand rests on sword-back, blade-edge forward, point down. Gaze on opponent.

b) A carries straight on. Pivoting on both feet, A turns right a complete revolution, sword following round in a Level Swipe. Gaze on B's sword.

B carries straight on. Pivoting on both feet, B turns right a complete revolution, Upright Sword following turn pushing forward and right. Gaze on A. (Diag. G. 13)

Essentials:

Both sides must turn simultaneously. Swipe and Push must have outward momentum, extending well out from body. Turns must be swift, both sides nimbly adjusting their feet as necessary.

14) A ... Bow Stance with Downward Hack
B ... Knee Raise with Cut to Wrist

A turns a complete revolution. Right leg does not move, left leg extends straight to rear(W), right leg bending to half squat to form Right Bow Stance. At same time, as

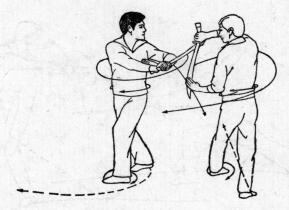

Diag. G. 13

left leg extends out to rear, sword hacks at B's right leg. Left palm is extended out level to rear. Gaze on B's leg.

B turns a complete revolution. Seeing A hack at right leg, he swiftly passes left leg in front of right leg to right side in Covering Step, toes pulled in, right knee raised up in front of body. At same time, sword cuts down to A's right wrist. Left palm rests on right forearm. Gaze on A's wrist. (Diag. G.14)

Essentials:

After both sides turn, A's hack to leg and B's cut to wrist must be completed together. Hack to leg should be close, regulated by size of A's Bow Stance.

15) A ... Step Forward with Sword Push
  B ... Step Forward and Lean Back

A steps forward with left foot(E), knee bending to form Left Bow Stance. At same time, right forearm turns out so wrist faces up, and sword swings left, up, past front of body to right to above B's right arm, blade-edge forward,

Diag. G. 14

point right. Left palm rests on right wrist, finally executing a straight arm Sword Push towards B's neck. Gaze on B's head.

B's right foot lands in front of body, left foot then takes a step forward(W). Torso leans back. At same time, right forearm turns out, wrist hooking in so blade-edge faces left, point up, sword positioned in front of body, so sword-face blocks A's Push. Left hand rests on right wrist. Gaze on A. (Diag. G.15)

Essentials:

A first pushes, B then blocks. Direction of Push must be obliquely upward and B must use sword-face to obliquely block A's sword.

16) A ... Rest Stance Turning Body to Hack at Leg
B ... Cross Stance Turning Body to Cut at Wrist

A carries straight on. Right foot takes a step forward (E), toes turned out, both legs bending to full squat to

Diag. G. 15

form Rest Stance. At same time, torso turns right so blade-edge hacks at B's legs. Left palm moves out to upper left in Palm Push. Gaze on B's legs.

B carries straight on. Right foot takes a step forward (W), knee bending to half squat to form Cross Stance with left leg straightened. At same time, torso turns to right rear, blade-edge swiftly cutting A's right wrist. Left palm is raised up to upper left. Gaze on A's wrist. (Diag. G.16)

Essentials:

Movements (15) and (16) must be continuous. If B's cut to wrist is too far away from A's wrist, then one can change to a cut to A's sword. The distance between the two sides can be adjusted by agile footwork.

17) A ... Turn with Entwining the Head

B ... Turn, Step Forward and Chop

Pivoting on balls of both feet, B turns right round to left, then takes a step forward with right foot(E), knee

Diag. G. 16

bending to half squat, left leg straightening to form Right
Bow Stance. At same time, following turn of body, sword
swings right round horizontally with blade-edge forward
in a level Chop to A's neck. Left palm is raised level out
to left side. Gaze on A's head.

Pivoting on balls of both feet, A turns 270° to left rear
(chest facing North), legs forming Parallel Open Stance.
At same time, following turn of body, right arm raises
sword left and up past left shoulder in an Entwining the
Head, so that when B chops, A uses his sword behind his
back to block B's sword. Left palm is withdrawn to in
front of right chest. Gaze on B. (Diag. G.17)

Essentials:

Both sides must turn togeher. A's Entwining the Head
must be perfectly timed to meet B's Chop.

18) A . . . **Kneel with Sweep**
 B . . . **Knee Raise with Embracing**

A brings sword round right shoulder to right, then forward and down with straight arm. At this point, torso

310

Diag. G. 17

turns left, left foot taking a half step to front left (S-W). Right leg kneels on ground, sword sweeping at B's right leg. Left palm is raised level out to left side. Gaze on sword-body.

B's sword continues from Chop to A's head to left, coming to rest on the left arm, blade-edge out, point to rear. Left palm rests on right wrist. When A sweeps at right leg, B swiftly raises leg in a Knee Raise. Gaze on A. (Diag. G.18)

Essentials:

Movements (17) and (18) must be continuous. A's Sweep must not be extended too far in case sword strikes B's supporting leg.

19) A . . . Knee Raise with Chop
     B . . . Kneel with Sweep

B's right foot lands to right front(S-E), knee bending to half squat, left leg kneeling on ground. At same time, with left palm resting on right wrist, right hand swings sword

311

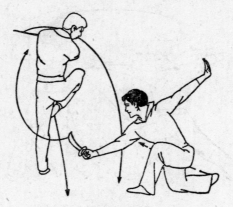

Diag. G. 18

down from left in a Sweep at A's lower limbs. Gaze on A's legs.

A stands up, sees B sweeping down and supports body on left leg. Right leg is swiftly raised up in Knee Raise. At same time, right forearm turns inward so blade-edge faces right, Swinging Sword in a Reverse Chop to B's head. Left palm is raised level at left side. Gaze on B. (Diag. G.19)

Essentials:

B's right foot landing and Downward Sweep should be completed together, as should A's Knee Raise and Chop.

20) A ... Cross Stance with Concealing
B ... Cross Stance with Concealing

A's right foot lands to right front (N-W), toes turned out, knee bending to half squat. Left leg straightens, heel rising up to form Cross Stance. At same time, straight right arm pulls sword to right rear to form Concealing, blade-edge down, point forward. Left palm pushes out

Diag. G. 19

forward to form Upright Palm, wrist connecting with B's
left wrist. Gaze on B.

B rises up swiftly, left leg straightening, heel rising up,
right leg bent at knee, toes turned out to form Cross
Stance. At same time, right forearm turns in, arm pulling
sword back to right rear to form Concealing, blade-edge
down, point forward. Left palm pushes out to front to
form Upright Palm, wrist connecting with A's left wrist.
Gaze on A. (Diag. G.20)

Essentials:

Both sides' Cross Stance with Concealing must form a
straight line, A to East, B to West. Both sides should
adjust their footwork to ensure the correct distance
between them. Both sides' movements must be completed
together.

21)   A ...   Horse Stance with Stab
   B ...   Horse Stance with Stab

A takes a step forward with left foot(N-W), torso turn-

Diag. G. 20

ing left. Right foot then takes a step forward(E), both legs bending to half squat to form Horse Stance. At same time, right hand thrusts sword past waist in a Level Stab at B's left ribs, blade-edge down, point right. Left palm is raised level to left side. Head turns right, gaze forward.

B takes a step forward with left foot(E), torso turning left. Right foot then takes a step forward(E), both legs bending to half squat to form Horse Stance. At same time, right hand thrusts sword past waist in a Level Stab at A's left ribs, blade-edge down, point right. Left palm is raised level out to left side. Head turns right, gaze forward. (Diag. G.21)

Essentials:

Both sides must face each other, their movements identical, and completed together. They must not be too far apart, the distance being adjusted by the step forward with left foot.

22) A . . . **Step Forward with Sweep Thrust**
     B . . . **Step Forward with Sweep Thrust**

Diag. G. 21

A turns torso to left. Left toes turn out. Both legs straighten, weight shifting forward to form Front Back Open Stance with right heel raised. At same time, right hand swings sword down, left and forward in a Sweep Thrust, blade-edge up, point forward. Left palm is extended straight up, palm in. Gaze on sword-point.

B's movements are the same as A's. (Diag. G.22)
Essentials:
Both sides' movements must be uniform.

23) A ... Cross Stance with Concealing
**   B ... Cross Stance with Concealing**

a) A takes a step forward with right foot(E), toes turned in. Torso turns to left rear(W), left toes turning out, weight shifting forward onto left foot, right heel rising up. At same time, right hand raises sword up above head, blade-edge forward, point up. Left palm swings down to beside left waist, palm down. Gaze on opponent.

B's movements are the same as A's. (Diag. G.23.1)

b) Carrying straight on. A takes a step back with left foot(E), leg straight, heel raised. Right leg bends to half

Diag. G. 22

Diag. G. 23.1

squat to form Cross Stance. At same time, right hand
swings sword forward, down and to right rear to form

Concealing, blade-edge down, point forward. Left palm pushes out in front of chest to form Upright Palm. Gaze on opponent.

B's movements are the same as A's (Diag. G.23.2)

Diag. G. 23.2

Essentials:

Both sides' movements must be uniform.

24) A ... **Bow Stance with Stab**

    B ... **Twist with Vertical Slash**

A steps forward with left foot, then takes another step forward with right foot(W), knee bending to half squat, left leg straightening to form Right Bow Stance. At same time, right hand thrusts sword at B's head in a Stab. Left palm swings round to rear, fingers up, Gaze on sword-point.

B turns torso to left. Right leg straightens to form Parallel Open Stance. At same time, right hand brings sword up in front of body to form Upright Sword, then slashes to left to block A's Stab with the sword-face, blade-edge left, point up. Left palm rests on right wrist. Gaze on A's sword. (Diag. G.24)

Essentials:

When B sees A stab he then swiftly twists body to parry. The Vertical Slash used as a parry should meet the attack

Diag. G. 24

with the blade-edge, but this is changed to the sword-face
in duel routines to prevent damage to the blade-edge.

25) A ... Forward Leap to Rest Stance with Downward Cut
B ... Turning Leap to Bow Stance with Stab

a) B's weight shifts left, torso turning to left rear(E).
Left foot leaps off ground, the back leg following the turn
and swinging out to rear. At same time, following turn,
right hand brings sword up, forward and down, blade-
edge down, point forward. Left palm swings in opposite
direction, down and then up and out to left side, palm
down. Gaze forward.

A takes a small step with left foot to just in front of
right foot, then immediately leaps forward off ground,
right leg to fore, left leg bending up behind right knee. At
same time, right forearm turns outward, bent arm raised
up in front of head, sword horizontal, blade-edge up,
point to right. Left palm rests on right forearm. Gaze on
sword-body. (Diag. G.25.1)

Diag. G. 25.1

b) B's right foot lands on ground (E). Left foot lands to rear of right leg(W), leg straightening to form Right Bow Stance. At same time, right hand thrusts sword with straight arm at A's lower parts in a Downward Stab. Left palm is raised up to left side. Gaze on A.

A's right foot lands on ground(W). Left foot lands behind right foot(N-W), both legs bending to full squat to form Rest Stance. At same time, right hand swings sword left, down and forward in a Cut, blade-edge forward, point out, blocking B's Stab. Left palm is raised up to left side. Gaze on B's sword. (Diag. G.25.2)

Essentials:

Both sides must leap together. A should observe the distance of B's Turning Leap and adjust his Forward Leap accordingly so that B can stab with straight arm. Stab

Diag. G. 25.2

and Cut should be completed together.

26) A... Advancing Step with Sweep Thrust
B... Kneel and Parry

A straightens up, and pivoting on the balls of both feet turns round to left rear. Left foot then takes a big step forward(W), left leg slightly bent, right leg straight. At same time, right hand follows turn, forearm turning in, lifting sword-hilt up, so blade-edge is forward, point slanting down to form Upright Sword, swinging up in a Reverse Sweep Thrust to B's chest. Left palm rests on right forearm. Gaze on B.

B sees A's sword sweeping up towards his chest and retreats a step with right foot (W), knee bending to kneel on ground. Left foot takes a step forward, knee bending to half squat, torso leaning back. At same time, B bends right wrist so sword is brought horizontal across chest, left palm resting on sword-back, blade-edge up, point left, reaching up to block A's Sweep Thrust. Gaze on A. (Diag. G.26)

320

Diag. G. 26

Essentials:

A's advancing step and B's retreating step must be co-ordinated. Parry and Sweep Thrust must move up together. A's sword should be as upright as possible, so as to avoid the point striking the opponent.

27) A ... Step Forward with Downward Stab

B ... Knee Raise with Left Side Press

A takes a step forward with right foot(W), knee bending slightly. At same time, right hand withdraws sword to beside waist, blade-edge down, point forward, then swiftly stabs at B's left leg. Left palm leaves right forearm and swings past waist out level to left side, fingers up, palm facing out. Gaze on sword-point.

B straightens up, right leg supporting body-weight. Left knee rises up in front of body. At same time, right hand turns sword-point down, blade-edge forward in a Side Press to left side. Left palm rests on right wrist. Gaze on A's sword. (Diag. G.27)

Diag. G. 27

Essentials:

A withdraws sword and left palm to waist before stepping forward. Stab and step should be completed together.

28) A ... T-Stance with Withdrawl of Sword
**   B ... Falling Step with Raised Sword**

A withdraws right foot to left instep, both legs bending to half squat to form T-Stance. At same time, right arm bends so gripping palm faces in in front of chest, blade-edge up, point forward. Left palm rests on right wrist. Gaze on B.

B turns round left to rear(N), left foot landing to left (W) to form Parallel Open Stance. At same time, right wrist bends so sword-point swings back past left side and up until sword is raised with bent arm in front of head, blade-edge up, point right. Left palm rests on right wrist. Head turns right, gaze on A. (Diag. G.28)

Diag. G. 28

Essentials:

B continues straight on from previous Side Press up into raised sword.

29) A ... Bow Stance with Stab
**   B ... Right Side Press**

A steps forward with right foot(W), knee bending to half squat, left leg straightening to form Right Bow Stance. At same time, right forearm turns, thrusting out at B's lower right leg in a Downward Stab, blade-edge down, point forward. Left palm leaves right wrist and swings out to left side, fingers up, palm facing out. Gaze on B's leg.

B raises right knee up in front of body, left heel turning out, torso turning slightly to right. At same time, right hand swings sword in an arc forward, right and down in a Side Press, blade-edge forward, point down, parrying A's Stab. Left palm still rests on right wrist. Gaze on A's sword. (Diag. G.29)

Diag. G. 29

Essentials:

A's Stab and Bow Stance must be completed together.
B's Side Press must be inside A's blade, torso leaning
forward slightly.

30) A ... Covering Step with Downward Hack

B ... Turn to Covering Step and Vertical Slash

A's torso turns left. Left foot takes a half step forward,
heel raised. Right foot then takes a Covering Step past
left leg out to left side, toes turned out to form a small
Cross Stance. At same time, right forearm turns out,
sword swinging up, at which point the arm bends. Left
palm rests on right wrist, then sword continues swing left,
down and right in a Hack to B's legs. Left palm again
leaves right wrist and pushes out to upper left to form
Exposed Palm. Head turns right, gaze on sword-point.

B's right foot lands to right side, toes turned out. Left
foot then passes right leg in Covering Step to right side(W),

toes turned out, torso turning right in accordance. At same time, left palm leaves right wrist and swings left, up and right. Right hand swings sword right up, left and down in a Vertical Slash, parrying A's Hack. Left palm rests back on right wrist. Gaze on sword-body. (Diag. G.30)

Diag. G. 30

Essentials:
Both sides' movements must be coordinated and completed together. A should twist body to right rear during Hack, B should twist to left rear during Slash, both blades making contact, A's sword outside B's.

31)   A . . .   T-Stance with Parry
B . . .   Backward Cross Stance with Parry

A's torso turns left to rear(N), toes of right foot turning in to face North. Left foot is withdrawn in to right instep, toes touching ground, both legs bent to half squat to form T-Stance. At same time, following turn, right hand swings sword forward, then once in front of body, up above head in a Parry, blade-edge up, point left. Left arm bends, bringing palm in in front of right shoulder. Gaze on opponent.

Pivoting on balls of both feet, B turns right a full revolution, both legs straight, right leg in front, left leg behind to form a small Cross Stance. At same time, following turn, right hand swings sword with blade-edge out in a circle for a full revolution, then up above the head in a Parry, blade-edge up, point to left. Left palm moves up to in front of right shoulder. Gaze on opponent. (Diag. G.31)

Diag. G. 31

Essentials:

Both sides must turn, Parry and look together. A is East, B is West.

32) A ... Retreating Step with Sweep Thrust

B ... Step Forward with Sweep Thrust

B takes a step forward(E) with left foot, toes turned out.

Right foot immediately takes another step forward, leg slightly bent. At same time, right hand swings sword back, down and forward in a Sweep Thrust with blade-edge up to A's left side. Left palm swings out to upper rear. **Gaze on sword-body.**

A turns left. Right toes turn in, left foot takes a step back, toes turned out, right leg slightly bent. At same time, right hand swings sword back, down and forward in a Sweep Thrust to meet B's blade. Left palm rests on right forearm. Gaze on B's sword. (Diag. G.32)

Diag. G. 32

Essentials:

Both sides must Sweep Thrust together, blades touching.

33) A ... Retreating Step with Sweep Thrust

B ... Step Forward with Sweep Thrust

Carry straight on. B takes a step forward with left foot(E), leg slightly bent. At same time, right hand swings sword with bent arm left, down and forward, forearm turning in so gripping palm faces up, in a Sweep Thrust with reverse wrist. Left palm rests on right wrist. Gaze on A's arm.

A takes a step backward with right foot(E), left leg bends slightly. At same time, carrying straight on from above Sweep Thrust, bent right arm swings up, left, down and forward, forearm turning in, gripping palm up in a Sweep Thrust with reverse wrist at B. Left palm rests on right forearm. Gaze on B's sword. (Diag. G.33)

Diag. G. 33

Essentials:

Both sides must Sweep Thrust together, A's blade inside B's. The blades can make contact.

34) A ... Turning Leap to Bow Stance with Downward Stab

B .. Leap to Rest Stance with Downward Cut

a) Carry straight on. A turns torso left (facing S).

Left foot takes a stride out to left(E). At same time, right forearm turns out so blade-edge faces up, point left, sword raised level above head in a Parry. Left palm follows turn of body and leaves right forearm, swinging down and left, so palm faces forward. Head turns left, gaze forward.

B shifts weight right, withdrawing left foot to in front of right foot in a Point Stance. At same time, right hand brings sword up and right to form Upright Sword at right side, blade-edge right, point up. Gaze on A. (Diag. G.34.1)

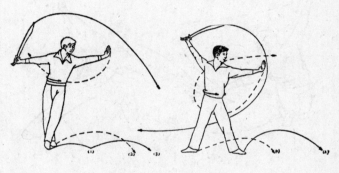

Diag. G. 34.1

b) Carry straight on. A turns torso left (facing E), leaping off ground with left foot. Right foot takes a stride forward(E), toes pulled in, torso continuing to turn to left rear(W). Left foot lands behind body, leg straight, right leg bending to half squat to form Right Bow Stance. At same time, following turn of body, right hand brings sword up, left and down past waist and forward in a level Stab at B, blade-edge down, point forward. Left palm follows turn and swings down, left, up and to rear, fingers up. Gaze on sword-point.

B turns torso left. Left foot shifts left, then springs off ground. Right foot strides forward(E), toes turned in on landing. Left foot immediately lands behind right foot, both legs bending to full squat to form Rest Stance. At same time, following leap, right hand brings sword up, left, down, and forward in a Cut to block A's Stab, blade-edge slanting down, point left. Left palm is raised to upper left. Head turns right, gaze on A. (Diag. G.34.2)

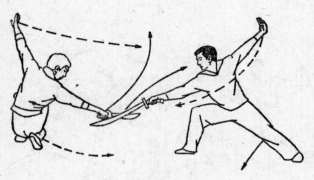

Diag. B. 34.2

Essentials:

A must leap first, B following, therefore B must adjust the distance between them with his leap so that the movement can be smoothly executed.

35) A . . . Kneel and Parry

B . . . Step Forward with Sweep Thrust

B straightens up, torso turning slightly right. Right foot takes a step forward(E), leg slightly bent. At same time, right forearm turns in, hilt raised up so point is down, blade-edge forward, swinging up in a Sweep Thrust in front of A's chest. Left palm rests on right wrist. Gaze on opponent.

A shifts weight back, left knee kneeling on ground, torso leaning back. At same time, right wrist bends to bring sword horizontal in front of chest, left palm on sword-back, blade-edge up, point left, following B's Sweep Thrust up and back in a Parry. Gaze on B's sword. (Diag. G.35)

Diag. G. 35

Essentials:

B's Sweep Thrust comes first, A leaning back and parrying in response. B's sword must be vertical during Sweep Thrust, the point not stuck out, in order to avoid injury to A. Parry should follow the momentum of the Sweep Thrust.

36)　A ... Kneel and Sweep
　　　B ... Leap with Level Chop

Carry straight on. A takes a large step with left foot to front left(S-W), knee bending to half squat. Right leg kneels on ground. Left palm leaves sword-back and is raised to upper left rear. Right hand swings sword right, down and forward in a Sweep at B's legs. Gaze on B's feet.

B sees A's Sweep to legs, and swiftly withdraws right foot to alongside left, then leaps forward with both feet, bending the legs in mid-air. At same time, B spins wrist so sword makes a small revolution left, back and right, then chopping at A's head. Left palm is raised level to left side. Gaze on A. (Diag. G.36)

Diag. G. 36

Essentials:

Sweep must be close to the ground. Both sides' movements must be coordinated. Leap must be to East and long, so A and B change positions.

37)   A . . .   Mid-air Backward Slice
 B . . .   Bow Stance with Stab

B lands on ground and immediately turns round to right rear, right leg bent to half squat, left leg straightened to form Right Bow Stance. At same time, right hand thrusts sword swiftly at A's torso in a Stab, blade-edge down. Left palm follows turn of body, raised up level to rear. Gaze on A.

After sweeping at B's legs, A takes another step forward with right foot(W), then leaps off ground, knees bent, turning right in mid-air, left leg swinging left and to rear to form mid-air Right Bow Stance. At same time, right hand swings sword left, up and forward in a Slice at B's head(E). Gaze on B. (Diag. G.37)

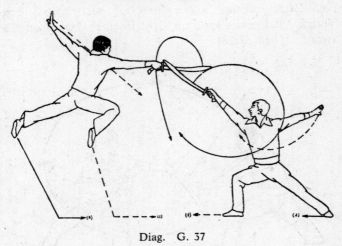

Diag. G. 37

Essentials:

A's step forward, leap and turn must be quick and not too far. Both sides' speed must be coordinated so sword movements are performed together.

38) A ... Horse Stance with Downward Cut
    B ... Horse Stance with Downward Sweep Thrust

B shifts right foot forward(W). Left foot follows suit,

333

both legs bending to half squat to form Horse Stance (facing S). At same time, right forearm turns out, wrist spinning up so sword swings up, past front of body, down and forward at A in a Sweep Thrust, blade-edge forward, point down. Left palm rests on right forearm. Gaze on A.

A's feet land (chest facing N). Right foot takes a stride right, left foot following with a half step, both legs bending to half squat to form Horse Stance. At same time, right hand raises sword up in front of body, blade-edge forward, point left, then brings it down in a Cut to parry B's Sweep Thrust. Left palm rests on right forearm. Gaze on B's sword. (Diag. G.38)

Diag. G. 38

Essentials:

B shifts forward and Sweep Thrusts only after he sees A landing. When A sees B striking he swiftly shifts right and Cuts to parry B's Sweep Thrust.

39) A ... Cross Stance with Upward Parry
B ... Step Forward to Brandishing Slice

B raises right foot, toes turn out, foot then stamps down in original position. Torso follows stamping foot and turns right. Left foot takes a step forward, knee bends to half squat, right leg straightens to form Left Bow Stance. At same time, right hand swings sword down, past right side of body to rear, up and forward in a Slice with blade-edge at A's head. As torso turns right with stamp, left palm swings out level to left side. Gaze on A.

A straightens up, torso turning 180° to right rear(to face S). Right foot rises up, toes turn out and foot lands on ground, leg slightly bent, left leg straightening to form a small Cross Stance. At same time, following turn of torso, right hand swings sword up to parry B's Slice, blade-edge up, point left. Left palm remains on right forearm. Head turns left, gaze on B's sword. (Diag. G.39)

Essentials:

Diag. G. 39

B slices first, A then parries. Both sides must co-ordinate timing.

40) A ... Left Upward Kick

      B ... Loss of Sword

A turns right toes out, and with right leg supporting body, kicks forward and up with left foot, toes striking B's right elbow. Gaze on B's arm.

B's right arm is kicked by A, the sword dropping out of his grip. (Diag. G.40)

Diag. G. 40

Essentials:

A's Spring Kick should not be too powerful, but should connect with B's right arm. B must coordinate kick with releasing his sword. A should lean torso to right when kicking, making sure that the kick is accurate.

41) A ... Land with Embracing

      B ... Step Forward with Side Spring Kick

After B loses sword, he takes a step forward with right foot (W), toes turning out, torso also turning right. At same time, right palm turns to fist and left palm rests on right wrist. Head turns left, gaze on A.

After Spring Kick, A's left foot lands to left side of body(N) to form Front-back Open Stance. At same time, right hand follows turn and swings sword right past front of body and left to below left ribs, blade-edge out, point to left rear. Left arm bends in front of chest. Head turns right, gaze on B. (Diag. G.41.1)

Diag. G. 41.1

B carries straight on. Right leg supports body, torso turns right and leans back to right. Left foot, toes pointed straight, kicks up at A's waist with flat of foot. Gaze on A. (Diag. G.41.2)

Essentials:

B's step forward with right foot must be so adjusted to ensure that he can strike A's waist when kicking.

42) A ... **Back Drop**

B ... **Right Outward Swing Kick**

a) Carry straight on. When A is kicked on the waist, torso immediately leans forward and to left and right leg bends up behind body.

B's left foot lands in front of body(E), toes turned in, torso turning round to right. Right foot swings forward and right in an Outward Swing Kick. Both palms strike face of right foot. (Diag. G.42.1)

Diag.   G. 41.2

b) A carries straight on. Torso bends down, head tucked in, waist bent, with first the right shoulder, then back, waist and backside landing on ground, rolling forward(N-W) in a Back Drop. Once roll is completed, A comes up to kneel on right leg.

B's right foot lands to right rear (S-E), leg straight. Left leg bends to half squat to form Left Bow Stance. Right palm strikes out forward past waist in a Finger Thrust, palm up, fingers forward. Left palm turns to fist and is withdrawn to waist, knuckles down. Gaze on A. (Diag. G.42.2)

Essentials:

A's Back Drop and roll must be performed at the same time as B's Kick. A's roll and B's Bow Stance must be

Diag. G. 42.1

Diag. G. 42.2

completed at same time.

43) A ... Turn to Bow Stance with Concealing
      B ... Palm Push to Attention

a) A stands up, torso turning round to right rear(E).

Left leg supports body, right knee raised up. At same time, right hand raises sword forward, right and up to perform Binding the Head, blade-edge to rear, point down. Left palm is withdrawn to in front of right chest. Gaze on B.

B's left leg straightens and shifts back a half pace to form Front-Back Open Stance. Left fist turns to palm and thrusts forward, palm up, to above right palm. Gaze on A. (Diag. G.43.1)

Diag. G. 43.1

b) A turns torso slightly to right, and right foot lands to right side(S-W), knee bending to half squat, left leg straightening to form Right Side Bow Stance. At same time, right hand pulls sword round to right rear to form Concealing, blade-edge down, point forward. Left palm strikes out towards B in Palm Push, fingers up. Head turns left, gaze on B.

B's right foot coming up beside left to form Attention

Stance (chest facing N). Right palm turns to fist and is withdrawn to waist, knuckles down. Left palm strikes out to left in Palm Push, fingers up, side of little finger forward. Gaze on A. (Diag. G.43.2)

Essentials:

Both sides must finish together, and should basically end up where they started.

If one wishes to continue straight on to the next routine (barehand vs. sword), then there is no need to perform the closing posture, but carry straight on from Diag. G.43.

Diag. G. 43.2

Dual Routine II:

1) A ... Embracing to Attention
   B ... Saluting to Attention
2) A ... Step Forward with Hand Parry and Hack
   B ... Step Forward with Hand Parry and Duck Head

3) A . . . Reverse Chop
   B . . . Bend Over Backward
4) A . . . Step Forward and Parry with Fist
   B . . . Rise up and Parry with Palm
5) A . . . Bend Forward and Duck Head
   B . . . Inward Kick with Right Foot
6) A . . . Left Side Stamp Kick
   B . . . Turn and Lean Back
7) A . . . Striking Step
   B . . . Back Drop
8) A . . . Step Forward and Raise Sword
   B . . . Half Horse Stance with Palm Push
9) A . . . Step Forward with Left Slice
   B . . . Retreating Step with Right Covering Palm
10) A . . . Right Slice
    B . . . Left Covering Palm
11) A . . . Reverse Step and Shrink Chest
    B . . . Horse Stance with Palm Push
12) A . . . Sweep
    B . . . Leap
13) A . . . Reverse Chop
    B . . . Land and Duck Head
14) A . . . Left Reverse Forearm Smash
    B . . . Grip Wrist and Support Elbow
15) A . . . Lean Forward Whilst Gripped
    B . . . Step Forward and Press on Shoulder
16) A . . . Empty Stance with Open Arms
    B . . . Open Stance with Open arms
17) A . . . Reverse Step with Hack
    B . . . Palm Push and Lean Forward
18) A . . . Leap with Level Chop
    B . . . Press on Floor with Leg Sweep
19) A . . . Step Forward with Downward Hack

	B ...	Lean Forward and Duck Head
20)	A ...	Downward Sweep
	B ...	Lean Forward and Spring into Air
21)	A ...	Downward Slice
	B ...	Legs Thrust Through Middle
22)	A ...	Sweep
	B ...	Retract Legs and Roll Backwards
23)	A ...	Reverse Sweep
	B ...	Carp Flips Erect
24)	A ...	Leap and Raise Sword
	B ...	Forward Leg Sweep
25)	A ...	Lean Back with Raised Sword
	B ...	Rear Outward Leg Swing
26)	A ...	Bent Arm Is Gripped
	B ...	Push Elbow and Press Wrist
27)	A ...	Loss of Sword
	B ...	Rids Opponent of Sword
28)	A ...	Gripped by Opponent
	B ...	Push to Cheek
29)	A ...	Grips Opponent
	B ...	Gripped by Opponent
30)	A ...	Low Leg Hook
	B ...	Fall onto Left Side
31)	A ...	Forward Leap and Roll
	B ...	Black Dragon Entwining Pillar
32)	A ...	Fistfight Stance
	B ...	Fistfight Stance
33)	A ...	Footwork
	B ...	Footwork
34)	A ...	Right Fist-block
	B ...	Right Fist-block
35)	A ...	Left Fist-block
	B ...	Left Fist-block

36)	A . . .	Retreating Step with Double Parry
	B . . .	Step Forward with Right Fist Slice
37)	A . . .	Turn with Double Parry
	B . . .	Turn with Left Fist Slice
38)	A . . .	Retreating Step with Foot Slap
	B . . .	Collect Fists with Spring Kick
39)	A . . .	Turn to Leap with Foot Slap
	B . . .	Step Forward to Leap with Forward Spring Kick
40)	A . . .	Advancing Step with Palm Press
	B . . .	Advancing Step with Straight Punch
41)	A . . .	Advancing Step with Palm Slice
	B . . .	Retreating Step with Supporting Palm
42)	A . . .	Inward Kick
	B . . .	Bend Forward
43)	A . . .	Rear Swing Kick
	B . . .	Turn to Parry with Forearms
44)	A . . .	Right Side Spring Kick
	B . . .	Shrink Chest to Guard Against Leg
45)	A . . .	Horse Stance with Downward Cross Palm
	B . . .	Horse Stance with Downward Cross Palm
46)	A . . .	Step Forward with Inward Kick
	B . . .	Step Forward with Inward Kick
47)	A . . .	Bow Stance with Twin Palm Chops
	B . . .	Bow Stance with Twin Palm Chops
48)	A . . .	Collect Hands to Attention
	B . . .	Collect Hands to Attention
49)	A . . .	Return to Starting Posture
	B . . .	Return to Starting Posture

Dual Routine   II:

The black-haired one is A, the white-haired one B.

1) A ... Embracing to Attention
**   B ... Saluting to Attention**

A Stands to Attention, legs straight, left heel placed at right instep, toes turned out. Torso turns slightly to left. Both arms raised up in front of chest, sword-gripping palm in, left palm resting on right forearm. Gaze on B.

B Stands to Attention, both legs straight, left heel placed at right instep, toes turned out. Torso turnes slightly to left. Both arms raised up bent in front of chest, left hand forming fist, knuckles facing in, right palm resting on face of left fist. Gaze on A. (Diag. H.1)

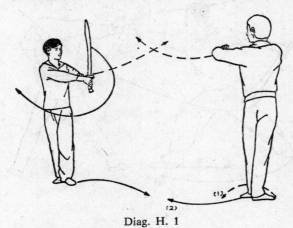

Diag. H. 1

2) A ... Step Forward with Hand Parry and Hack
**   B ... Step Forward with Hand Parry and**
**   Duck Head**

a) A takes a step forward with left foot(E), knee bending to half squat to form Left Bow Stance. Left palm extends forward, the back connecting with the back of B's palm. Right hand pulls sword back to form Concealing, blade-edge down, point forward. Gaze on B's palm.

B's right foot passes over left foot and lands to left, toes turned out, left foot then taking a stride to left(W) to form Parallel Open Stance. At same time, right palm turns to fist and is withdrawn to right waist. Left arm extends forward in a Palm Push, the back connecting with the back of A's palm. Gaze on A's wrist. (Diag. H.2.1)

Diag. H. 2.1

b) A first takes a half step back with left foot, right foot then taking a step forward(E, N-E), knee bending to half squat. Left foot immediately takes another step back(W), left leg straightening to form Right Bow Stance. At same time, right hand swings sword forward at B's head in a Hack. Left palm swings out to left side at shoulder height, fingers up. Gaze on B's head.

B sees A's Hack, bending body forward at waist and

ducking head down. Left palm turns to fist and is with-drawn to beside head, knuckles out. (Diag. H.2.2)

Diag. H. 2.2

Essentials:

Immediately after the left palms have connected, A hacks at B's head, sword close to B's back. B ducks head immediately after left palms connect.

3) A . . . Reverse Chop
B . . . Bend Over Backwards

A turns right forearm in so blade-edge faces right, then, seeing B straighten up, sweeps sword back at B's head in a Reverse Chop. Left palm is still raised out to left side. Gaze on B.

Having ducked the head, B swiftly straightens up, then seeing A's Reverse Chop, bends over backward, hands pressing on thighs. (Diag. H.3)

Essentials:

Diag. H. 3

A's first Hack must be long so as to give B time to straighten up. B must bend far over backward. A's Reverse Chop must stick close to B's chest, sweeping upward to avoid injury.

4) **A . . . Step Forward and Parry with Fist**
    B . . . Rise up and Parry with Palm

A takes a step back with right foot(W), left foot immediately stepping forward to behind B's left foot(E), to form Front-Back Open Stance. At same time, right hand pulls sword back to right rear to form Concealing. Left palm turns to fist, extending forward to connect with B's wrist. Gaze on B.

B straightens up, left foot raised, toes turning out to form Front-Back Open Stance. Left palm extends forward to connect with A's left wrist. Right arm bends, fist collected in at waist. Gaze on A's hand. (Diag. H.4)

    Essentials:

Diag. H. 4

Both sides must extend left arms simultaneously.

5) A... Bend Forward and Duck Head
B... Inward Kick with Right Foot

B shifts weight forward, right leg swinging up and to left, foot pulled in in an Inward Kick to A's Head. Once foot has passed A, left palm slaps sole of right foot. Gaze on A. A sees B's Kick and bends forward and ducks head, both arms swinging naturally in front of body. (Diag. H.5)

Essentials:

B's Kick should not be too high, and the slap can be omitted.

6) A... Left Side Stamp Kick
B... Turn and Lean Back

A straightens up and leans slightly to right, right leg supporting body, leg slightly bent. Left foot kicks left at the pit of B's back. Right hand holds sword in front

Diag. H. 5

of chest, left palm resting on right forearm. Gaze on B's waist.

B's right foot lands close to the left instep, torso turning left (to face E). Back faces A, arms bent up in front of chest. Since the back is kicked by A, B's weight shifts forward and torso leans back. Gaze forward. (Diag. H.6)

Essentials:

A kicks once B's back is turned.

7) A ... Striking Step
**   B ... Back Drop**

When kicked, B leaps forward, body bending forward, head tucked in, right shoulder landing first, then back, waist and backside, in a Back Drop Forward Roll.

A's left foot lands forward on ground, weight shifting forward. Left foot leaps off ground, right foot coming forward to strike left instep, so body flies forward in mid-air with feet together. At same time, right hand

Diag. H. 6

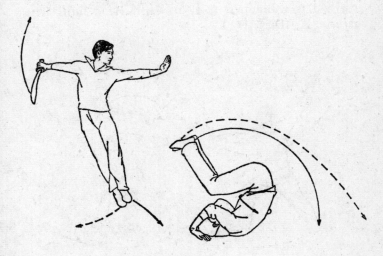

Diag. H. 7

pulls sword back to right rear to form Concealing. Left hand extends out forward in Palm Push. Gaze on B. (Diag. H.7)

Essentials:

A must adjust the speed and length of Striking Step according to speed and length of B's Back Drop.

8) A . . . Step Forward and Raise Sword

B . . . Half Horse Stance with Palm Push

A's right foot lands first, left foot then landing to fore, to form Open Stance with front leg bent and back leg straight. Right hand raises sword up so blade-edge is forward, point up. Left palm does not move. Gaze on B.

Rising up from the Back Drop, B immediately turns round left to face A. Left foot takes a pace forward(W), both legs bending to form Half Horse Stance. Left palm strikes out to left in Palm Push. Right palm turns to fist and is withdrawn to right waist. Head turns left, gaze on A. (Diag. H.8)

Diag. H. 8

Essentials:

A waits until B has turned before raising sword, so both complete their movements together.

9) A . . . Step Forward with Left Slice

B . . . Retreating Step with Right Covering Palm

A takes an arc step to S-E with left foot, toes turning out, right foot immediately taking a step forward(E), to form Front-Back Open Stance. At same time, right hand swings sword down in a Slice at the left of B's head. Left palm swings down and to rear. Gaze on sword-body.

B sees A's Slice and, pivoting on ball of right foot, takes a step back with left foot(E), torso turning left (to face S). Right fist turns to palm and swiftly moves down to catch A's right wrist. Left palm swings out to rear with turn. Gaze on A's hilt. (Diag. H.9)

Essentials:

A's Slice must be realistic and fast, B turning quickly, making sure to parry A's right wrist.

Diag. H. 9

10) A ... Right Slice
B ... Left Covering Palm

A carries straight on. Left foot takes a half step forward, right foot immediately taking another step forward to form Open Stance. Right hand swings sword down, left, back, up and forward in a Slice at the right side of B's head. Left palm does not move. Gaze on B.

B sees A's Slice and, pivoting on ball of left foot, takes a step back with right foot(E), toes turning out. Torso turns to right rear. Left palm swings up, forward and down to parry A's right wrist. Right palm swings back and up with turn. Gaze on A's hilt. (Diag. H.10)

Diag. H. 10

Essentials:

Both sides must keep close for the successive slices. The swing of the sword must be large.

11) A ... Reverse Step and Shrink Chest
B ... Horse Stance with Palm Push

a) A swings sword down and to right side, blade-edge forward, point up. At same time, right foot first takes a step to rear(W), left foot then shifting back a half step, to form Front-Back Open Stance. At this point, chest faces B, chest shrunk in as it is struck by B. Both arms are raised up level to sides of body.

B deliberately pulls A's right hand out to left with his left hand. Left toes turn out, right foot takes a step forward, toes turned in. Torso turns left (to face S), both legs bending to half squat to form Horse Stance. At same time, right hand passes waist and strikes forward at A's stomach with upright palm. Left palm rises left and up, palm up. Gaze on A. (Diag. H.11.1)

Diag. H.11.1

b) Having been struck by B, A retreats several paces, to form half Horse Stance, left foot forward, right foot to rear. Right hand raises sword up above head, blade-edge up, point forward. Left hand forms Upright Palm in front of body, fingers up. Gaze on B.

Having struck A, B bends legs to form Horse Stance, right hand extended forward, left hand still above head. (Diag. H.11.2)

Diag. H. 11.2

Essentials:

A must not retreat too far. B must hold the fixed posture after striking A.

12) A ... Sweep

B ... Leap

A takes two steps forward, finishing with right leg to fore, leg bent and torso leaning forward. At same time, right hand swings sword down in a Sweep at B's legs. Left arm is raised up to side. Gaze on sword-body.

B sees A sweep at legs and leaps off ground with both knees bent. Both arms are extended out to sides, palms down. Gaze on A's sword. (Diag. H.12.)

Essentials:

A can step forward as he likes, so long as right foot ends up to fore. Sweeping blade must be close to ground.

Diag. H. 12

13) A ... Reverse Chop
B ... Land and Duck Head

A's Sweep continues to the right, then right forearm turns in so blade-edge faces right. Seeing B land, A then swings sword to his head in a Reverse Chop. Left palm does not move. Gaze on B.

B lands on ground (facing S), legs apart. Arms in front of torso, elbows bent, torso bent forward, head tucked in. (Diag. H.13)

Essentials:

A's Reverse Chop must be perfectly coordinated with B's landing, B bending over once he sees the Chop coming.

14) A ... Left Reverse Forearm Smash
B ... Grip Wrist and Support Elbow

A takes a step forward in front of B's right leg with left foot(W). Right foot turns out, torso turns right(S).

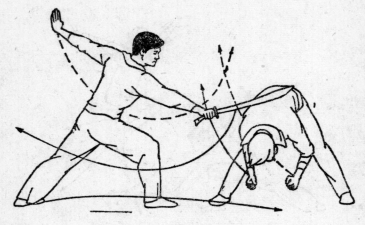

Diag. H. 13

At same time, right hand pulls sword back to right rear to form Concealing. Left palm turns to fist, then strikes forward past waist at B's face with back of knuckles. Gaze on B.

B straightens up, legs bending to half squat. Seeing A strike, he swiftly grasps A's wrist with his left hand, palm facing out, thumb down. Right palm supports A under left elbow, palm up. Gaze on right palm. (Diag. H.14)

Essentials:

B's two palms must grasp hold of A's arm simultaneously, after which, left palm turns over, right palm pushes up and out.

15)   A . . .   Lean Forward Whilst Gripped
B . . .   Step Forward and Press on Shoulder

B takes a step forward with left foot(S), landing in front of A's left leg, leg slightly bent. Left forearm turns in,

Diag. H. 14

pulling A's wrist down to in front of left chest. Right palm presses on A's elbow so A's arm straightens, then swiftly pushes down to left shoulder and presses down. Gaze on A.

Once A is gripped by B, weight shifts right. Right leg bends to half squat, left leg straightens and torso is forced forward and down. Right hand pulls sword up and back, point down. Head turns left, gaze on B. (Diag. H.15)

Essentials:

a) B should lean forward slightly, pressing down with right palm and lifting up with left.

b) A should follow B, deliberately leaning forward and straightening left arm, to avoid injury.

16)   A ...   **Empty Stance with Open Arms**
      B ...   **Open Stance with Open Arms**

a) A's feet do not move. Torso straightens up, waist

Diag. H. 15

Diag. H. 16.1

twisting left. Left elbow bends. At same time, A thrusts sword up under left armpit, so it is outside left arm, point up, blade-edge forward. Gaze on B.

360

B follows A's movements and straightens up. Hands still rest on A's left arm. Gaze on A. (Diag. H.16.1)

b) A carries straight on. Torso turns left, weight shifting to rear. Left foot shifts slightly backward, toes touching ground, both knees bending to form Empty Stance. At same time, right hand pushes sword forward, blade-edge forward. Left arm bends at elbow and pulls to rear. When blade-edge reaches elbow, the arms separate to left and right, blade-edge facing right so B is forced to release his grip. Both arms are then extended out level to sides, blade-edge right, point up. Left palm faces down. Gaze on B.

B is forced to release grip by A's sword and swiftly opens arms out to left and right with Upright Palms. Both legs bend slightly to form Parallel Open Stance. Gaze on A. (Diag. H.16.2)

Essentials:

Both sides must coordinate precisely, so when the

Diag. H. 16.2

sword pushes out to elbow they both open out to left and right together.

17) A ... Reverse Step with Hack
B ... Palm Push and Lean Forward

a) B raises right foot and stamps on ground. Left foot takes a large step forward, knee bending to half squat, right leg straightening to form Left Bow Stance. At same time, hands thrust past waist at A's stomach in twin Palm Push. Gaze on A.

A is struck by B's twin Palm Push and swiftly sinks the chest and draws in the stomach. (Diag. H.17.1)

Diag. H. 17.1

b) Having been struck, A takes a step back with left foot(W). Torso turns left. At same time, right hand swings sword forward in a Hack at B's head. Left palm swings out to rear, fingers up. Gaze on B.

B sees A's Hack and turns to right. Torso leans forward, both hands pressing on ground. Right leg extends

out to right side, left leg bending to full squat to form
Crouching Stance. Head turns left. Gaze on A. (Diag.
H.17.2)

Diag. H. 17.2

Essentials:

B stamps and pushes immediately after Open Arms.
A must be prepared to move, and once struck must step
back swiftly.

18) A ... Leap with Level Chop
B ... Press on Floor with Leg Sweep

B presses on floor with hands, left heel rising up. Right
leg sweeps round to rear at A's legs. Hands follow turn
in front of body. Gaze on A.

A carries straight on. Right forearm turns in so blade-
edge faces right, sweeping to rear in Level Chop. At
same time, both feet leap into the air, knees bent. Body
turns right in mid-air(E). Left palm is raised out to left
side. Gaze on B. (Diag. H.18)

Essentials:

Diag. H. 18

A's leap should have a rightward twisting force. B's Sweep should be fast, foot not leaving ground.

19) A ... Step Forward with Downward Hack
B ... Lean Forward and Duck Head

a) A lands and takes a step forward with right foot (E) to form Front-Back Open Stance. At same time, right arm bends to bring sword back onto right shoulder, blade-edge up, point to rear. Left palm rests on right forearm. Gaze on B.

B continues Leg Sweep to complete a full circle, chest now facing N. Legs straighten up, knees slightly bent, arms hanging by sides. Gaze on A. (Diag. H.19.1)

b) A carries straight on. Right leg bends forward, left leg straightening to form Right Bow Stance. At same time, right hand swings sword round and forward in a Hack at B's head. Left palm swings out level to left side. Gaze on B.

Diag. H. 19.1

B sees A's Hack and swiftly leans forward and ducks head, arms in front of chest with elbows bent. (Diag. H.19.2)

Essentials:

A Hacks after he sees that B has risen up. Hack must sweep across close to B's back.

20) A ...   Downward Sweep

B ...   Lean Forward and Spring into Air

A turns forearm in and reverses wrist, so blade-edge faces right, then sweeps down at B's legs. Left palm moves down to rest on right wrist. Gaze on B.

B stands up straight, and, seeing A's Sweep, leaps into the air with both feet, knees bent. Arms in front of body, palm down, gaze downward. (Diag. H.20)

Essentials:

A must time Sweep with B's leap so sword passes under body.

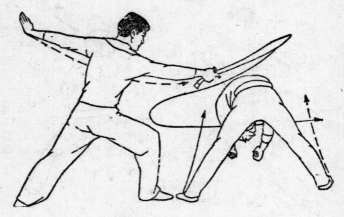

Diag. H. 19.2

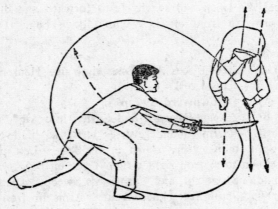

Diag. H. 2

21) A ... **Downward Slice**
   B ... **Legs Thrust Through Middle**

A's right foot shifts forward a half step (E), leg bending forward, left leg straightening to form Right Bow Stance. At same time, right hand swings sword back, up, forward and down in a Slice at B's legs, blade-edge down, point forward. Left palm swings out to left side. Gaze on B's legs.

B leans forward in mid-air, hands landing first, immediately bending arms and raising head, chest, stomach and legs then landing so whole body is lying face down flat on ground. On seeing A's Slice, B straightens arms to support body, raising the waist, pulling in the stomach and drawing in the legs so that the legs thrust through between the arms, finishing in a sitting position. (Diags. H.21.1,2,3)

Essentials:

A's Sweep and Slice must be regulated according to B's movements. One can lift one hand as the legs thrust through the middle of the arms.

Diag. H. 21.1

Diag.　H. 21.2

Diag.　H. 21.3

22)　A . . . Sweep
**　　　B . . . Retract Legs and Roll Backward**
　　A carries straight on. Right forearm turns out so blade-

edge faces left, sweeping along the ground at B's back-side. Gaze on B.

B leans torso back so shoulders and back touch ground. Legs swing up, body folding so legs pass above head. (Diag. H.22)

Diag. H. 22

Essentials:

A must coordinate with B so that sword passes under B's body as he leans back and raises legs.

23) A... Reverse Sweep

   B... Carp Flips Erect

A's right forearm turns in so blade-edge faces right, then sweeps along ground under B's back.

Having folded the body, B's hands rest on thighs (or floor), legs then thrust forward, up and down, immediately straightening stomach and raising body up with feet on ground. (Diag. H.23)

Essentials:

A must coordinate Sweep with B's flip, which must be fast. Flip can be done with hands pressing on ground

Diag. H. 23

above shoulders to provide extra force. A can shift feet as he wishes during successive Sweeps and can perform a few flourishes with the sword to lessen the waiting time.

24) A ... Leap and Raise Sword
B ... Forward Leg Sweep

a) After straightening up, B's left leg bends to full squat, heel raised, right leg extending straight out to side to form Crouching Stance. Arms then swing left, palms down. Gaze on A's legs.

A straightens up and withdraws right foot back to beside left, knees bent. At same time, right wrist bends, bringing sword left to rest on top of left arm. Left palm rests on right forearm. Gaze on B. (Diag. H.24.1)

b) B's hands rest on ground. Toes of right foot turn in, torso turning round to left rear, straight right leg sweeping round at A's legs. Head turns right, gaze on A.

Diag. H. 24.1

A leaps into the air, torso turning slightly to right, right leg bent in front of body, left leg extended to rear. At same time, right hand raises sword up, blade-edge to rear, point down. Left palm is raised level out to left side. Gaze on B. (Diag. H.24.2)

Essentials:

B must be close to A, so Sweep passes under A's feet. A leaps just before B's Sweep reaches his feet.

c) A lands on ground in Parallel Open Stance(E). Gaze on B. B sweeps until foot faces South, chest East, then withdraws right leg to form Parallel Open Stance, knees bent, torso bent forward slightly. Head twists round to left, gaze on A. (Diag. H.24.3)

Essentials:

B's Sweep must be fast and once chest faces East weight shifts right, legs forming Open Stance. A lands with sword raised as if about to slash down.

Diag. H. 24.2

Diag. H. 24.3

25)   A ...   Lean Back with Raised Sword
   B ...   Rear Outward Leg Swing

B's legs suddenly straighten, torso turning to left rear, right leg supporting body. Left leg swings up and to rear, aiming to strike A's head with heel. Arms extend out to sides. Head turns left, gaze on A.

A turns toes of both feet out, legs bending, weight shifting to rear and torso leaning back to avoid B's kick. Right hand swings sword to right side, left palm rising level at left side. Gaze on B's leg. (Diag. H.25)

Diag.   H. 25

Essentials:

B's turn and kick must be fast and not too high. A should lean back with straight waist, knees apart.

26)   A ...   Bent Arm Is Gripped
   B ...   Push Elbow and Press Wrist

   a) A raises sword ready to Slice at B's head. Gaze on B.

B turns to left rear (W), left foot landing outside A's right foot, leg bending forward. Arms move forward to grasp A's right arm, left hand gripping A's right wrist and pressing down, right palm lifting up under right elbow so A's right arm bends at elbow and he leans back. (Diag. H.26.1 and additional diagram)

b) B bends forward, left palm pressing down, right palm pushing forward, both arms extended.

A sinks to knees, leaning over backward. (Diag. H.26.2)

Diag. H. 26.1

c) A straightens legs with force, coming upright and pressing elbow forward trying to struggle free.

B straightens up and bends arms. (Diag. H.26.3) Same as Diag. H.26.1.

d) B bends torso forward, left palm pressing down, right palm pushing forward, both arms extended.

A sinks to knees, leaning over backward. (Diag. H.26.4) Same as Diag. H.26.2.

e) A straightens up, raising arm up straight with force, knees still on ground.

B straightens up and bends arms, left palm grasping

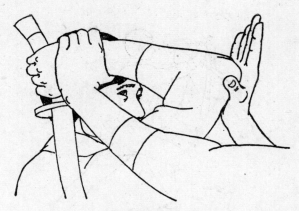

Additional Diagram

Diag. H. 26.2

A's right hand. Right palm presses against A's right elbow. (Diag. H.26.5)

Essentials:

Both sides must make it look like a fierce struggle.

Diag. H. 26.3

Diag. H. 26.4

The movements should be slow and steady.

27)   A ... Loss of Sword
      B ... Rids Opponent of Sword

376

Diag. H. 26.5

B pushes A's right elbow hard with right hand, left hand twisting out hard towards A's little finger, so that A's sword falls from hand. Gaze on opponent.

A leans over backward, right hand twisted open, the sword falling from his grip. (Diag. H.27)

Essentials:

Both sides must cooperate to make it look realistic.

28)   **A ...**   **Gripped by Opponent**
      B ...   **Push to Cheek**

B keeps a grip on A's wrist, continuing to twist left. Right palm pushes against A's left cheek.

A bends to right. Gaze on right palm. (Diag. H.28)

Essentials:

Left palm twists left and right palm presses cheek.

29)   **A ...**   **Grips Opponent**
      B ...   **Gripped by Opponent**

Diag. H. 27

Diag. H. 28

a) A bends left arm and presses down on B's right hand, the fingers gripping hold of his thumb.

B's right hand is gripped by A. (Diag. H.29.1)

Diag.   H. 29.1

b) A grips B's thumb and pulls it out to left, straightening arm and opening out wrist. At same time, legs straighten up, left foot taking a step out obliquely to left front, to form Front-Back Open Stance. Gaze on left palm.

B's right arm is pulled out straight, right leg bending slightly. Left leg straightens to form Parallel Open Stance. Gaze on right palm. (Diag. H.29.2)

Essentials:

When A presses down on B's right palm, the thumb presses down on the back of B's palm, while the fingers grasp his thumb and pull outward.

30)   A . . . Low Leg Hook
B . . . Fall onto Left Side

a) A's right toes turn in, right foot hooking round

Diag. H. 29.2   Diag. H. 30.1

behind B's left heel. Gaze on right wrist.

B raises right hand further up and shifts weight to left leg. (Diag. H.30.1)

b) A hooks away B's left heel with right foot. At same time, left hand pushes B down to right. Following Hook, torso turns right, arms extended out to both sides. Gaze on B.

B's left heel is hooked away by A, weight shifting left, feet leaving ground, body falling down to A's right side, legs in scissors position, bent left leg to fore, right leg extended straight to rear. Hands rest on ground. Gaze on A. (Diag. H.30.2)

Essentials:

a) Hook must catch opponent's heel, hook to left and push to right be executed together. b) When B is thrown, feet leave ground and body spins down to left.

Diag. H. 30.2

Outside of left leg lands first, then arms, right leg finally coming down to form scissors position. Fall must be to A's right side.

31) A ... Forward Leap and Roll
    B ... Black Dragon Entwining Pillar

a) B hooks in right foot and sweeps at A's left leg with straight leg.

A withdraws arms to straighten out in front of body, and, seeing B's Sweep, swiftly brings right foot back to beside left. (Diag. H.31.1)

b) A leaps forward for a forward roll.

B's right foot sweeps under A's feet off ground and torso starts to fall backward. (Diag. H.31.2)

c) A rolls forward into squatting position, hands resting on ground.

B's legs use the momentum of the Sweep with right leg to coil upward, at same time straightening the waist

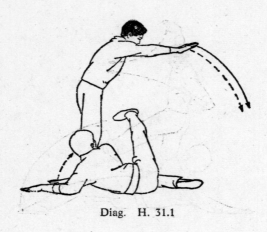

Diag. H. 31.1

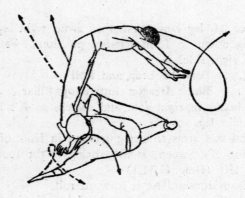

Diag. H. 31.2

and back, the hands pushing off the ground. (Diag.H.31.3)

d) Having spiralled upward, B then bends at middle, feet landing on ground so body stands upright facing N. A stands upright, facing E. (Diag. H.31.4)

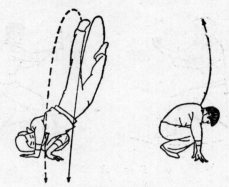

Diag. H. 31.3

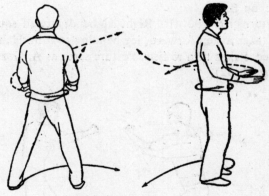

Diag. H. 31.4

32) A ... Fistfight Stance
B ... Fistfight Stance

A turns round to left rear(W), right leg bending to half squat, left foot taking a step forward(W), leg bending to half squat to form Half Horse Stance. Palms turn to fists,

Diag. H. 32

bent arms rising up in front of chest to form Fistfighting
Stance, left fist to fore, right fist level with left elbow.
Gaze on B.

B turns right 90° (E). Right leg bends to half squat, left
foot takes a step forward, leg bending to form Half Horse
Stance. Palms turn to fists. Posture same as A. Gaze on A.
(Diag. H. 32)

Diag. H. 33.1

Essentials:

Both sides must turn together.

33) A ... Footwork

B ... Footwork

A looks at B and, keeping left fist facing opponent, takes a series of arc steps forward starting with right foot until he reaches B's original position.

B does the same as A. (Diags. H. 33.1,2.)

Diag. H. 33.2

Both sides move in close, left legs to fore and bent to half squat, right legs extended to form Left Bow Stance (A facing E, B facing W). At same time, left arms extend out straight, fists turning to palms, backs of palms connecting. Right fists are pulled in to beside waist. Gaze on opponent. (Diag. H. 33.3)

Essentials:

Both sides can take as many steps as they wish, so long as they end up swapping positions. When pacing they must appear absolutely alert to their opponents' every

Diag. H. 33.3

move. Steps should not be too fast, both sides moving at same time.

34) A ... Right Fist-block
**   B ... Right Fist-block**

A takes a step back with left foot(W). At same time, right fist thrusts forward from waist and is blocked by B's right forearm, arm slightly bent, palm facing in towards body. Left palm turns to fist and is withdrawn to waist. Gaze on B.

B takes a step forward with right foot(W). At same time, right fist thrusts forward from waist and is blocked by A's right forearm, elbow slightly bent, palm facing in towards body. Left palm turns to fist and is withdrawn to waist. Gaze on A. (Diag. H. 34)

Essentials:

Both sides' movements must be completed together, sides of forearms connecting.

35) A ... Left Fist-block
**   B ... Left Fist-block**

Diag. H. 34

B takes a step forward with left foot(W), left fist thrusting forward from waist to be blocked by A's forearm, arm slightly bent, palm facing in. Right fist is withdrawn to waist. Gaze on left forearm.

A takes a step back with right foot(W), left fist thrusting forward from waist to be blocked by B's left forearm, arm slightly bent, palm facing in. Right fist is withdrawn to waist. Gaze on left forearm. (Diag. H. 35)

36) A . . . Retreating Step with Double Parry
B . . . Step Forward with Right Fist Slice

B takes a step forward with right foot(W), right fist swinging back, up, forward and down in a Slice towards A's head, knuckles right. Left fist is withdrawn to waist. Gaze on A's arms.

A takes a step back with left foot(W). Both fists turn to palms, forearms crossed in front of face, right arm on top of left, moving up to parry B's Fist Slice. Gaze on B's fist. (Diag. H.36)

Diag. H. 35

Diag. H. 36

37) A ... Turn with Double Parry

  B ... Turn with Left Fist Slice

Pivoting on right foot, B turns right 180° (facing N).

Left foot lands to left side(W). Left fist rises up from waist and swings down towards A's head in a Slice. Right fist is withdrawn to waist. Gaze on A.

A turns left, right foot taking a step to rear(W), toes pulled in, so body turns left a full revolution (chest facing E). During turn arms are withdrawn to stomach. After turn, arms cross, left on top of right, and thrust up to parry B's Slice. Gaze on B's fist. (Diag. H. 37)

Diag. H. 37

Essentials:
Both sides must turn swiftly and together. A sees B's Slice coming and then raises arms to parry.

38) A ...   Retreating Step with Foot Slap
B ...   Collect Fists with Spring Kick

B shifts weight onto left leg. Right foot stretches flat and swings up in a Spring Kick at A's stomach. At same time, left fist is withdrawn to waist. Gaze on A's hands.

A takes a step back with left foot(W). Left palm moves up on top of back of right palm, right hand moving down to slap the face of B's foot. Gaze on B's foot. (Diag. H.38)

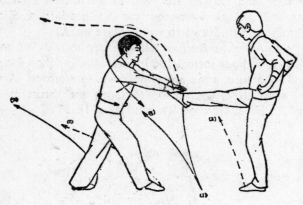

Diag. H. 38

Essentials:

B's kick should be to waist height. When A sees kick, he retreats and shrinks chest, slapping B's foot. The slap should be crisp and clear.

39) A ... Turn to Leap with Foot Slap

B ... Step Forward to Leap with Forward Spring Kick

a) B's right foot lands then leaps up into the air. Left leg bends in mid-air, right foot swiftly does another Spring Kick at A's stomach. Gaze on A.

Pivoting on ball of left foot, A starts to turn left and leaps off into the air. Left leg swings out to rear, body turning left a full revolution in mid-air. Right leg follows turn, bending up in front of body. In mid-air, right palm slaps B's right foot. Left palm swings out to rear. Gaze on B's foot. (Diag. H. 39.1)

b) B lands on both feet, right foot to fore, left foot to rear. Both fists remain at waist. Gaze on A.

Diag. H. 39.1

Diag. H. 39.2

A lands on both feet, right foot to fore, left foot to rear. Palms are withdrawn to sides. Gaze on B (Diag. H. 39.2)

Essentials:

Both sides must leap into the air at the same time, maintaining their respective distances so A can easly slap B's foot. Slap must be in mid-air.

40) A ... Advancing Step with Palm Press
**   B ... Advancing Step with Straight Punch**

B shifts right foot forward a half step(W), knee bending to half squat, left leg straightening to form Right Bow Stance. At same time, right fist strikes forward at A's chest. Left fist turns to palm and rests on inside of right forearm. Gaze on A's chest.

A takes a step forward with left foot(E), right foot shifting back a half step(W). Weight on right leg, both legs bent to form Half Horse Stance. At same time, left palm moves out to press down on B's right forearm, right palm still at waist. Gaze on B's arm. (Diag. H. 40)

Essentials:

A should shrink chest as he steps forward, so B's punch falls short, A then pressing down with palm.

Diag. H. 40

41) A ...   Advancing Step with Palm Slice
      B ...   Retreating Step with Supporting Palm

A takes a step forward(E) with right foot past the outside of B's right leg, left palm pressing B's right arm outward. At same time, right palm pushes out in a Slice at
B's head, palm forward, fingers up. Gaze on B's face.

B sees A's Slice coming and swiftly takes a step back
with right foot. Torso turns slightly to right and leans
back. Left palm, with thumb opened out, moves up to
support A's right palm. Gaze on A's hand. (Diag. H. 41)

Diag. H. 41

Essentials:
B's step back and palm support should be done together.

42) A ...   Inward Kick
      B ...   Bend Forward

A retracts right palm, palms turning to fists, arms swinging out to right side. Left foot shifts forward slightly, toes
turning out. Torso turns left, weight shifting to left leg.
Right leg swings up and in in an Inward Kick aiming to
kick B's head horizontally with face of foot. Gaze on B.

B takes a step back with right foot(E), retracting right fist and swiftly turning torso to right, bending forward and ducking head when A kicks. Arms placed naturally in front of body. (Diag. H. 42)

Diag. H. 42

Essentials:

A should shift his left foot forward according to the distance between himself and B so that right foot swings up exactly to B's head.

43) A . . . Rear Swing Kick
B . . . Turn to Parry with Forearms

a) A carries straight on. Kick passes over B's head, foot landing in front of B's left leg, toes turned in. Right fist comes forward in front of right side, left fist pulled in to waist. Gaze on B.

B swiftly straightens up, left fist moving out to left side, arm bent, right fist pulled in to waist. Head turns left, gaze on A. (Diag. H. 43.1)

b) Pivoting on ball of right foot, A turns left 180°,

Diag. H. 43.1

right leg straight, left leg swinging up to kick at B's chest with heel. Arms swing round following body, right arm extended straight up above head, left arm extended out straight to side. Gaze on B.

B sees A's kick and swiftly turns round to left rear, left foot landing on left side(E). Arms are bent up in front of chest, using sides of forearms to block A's kick. Gaze on A's leg. (Diag. H. 43.2)

Essentials:

A's right foot must land close to B's left side. After his turn, B must regulate his height according to the height of A's kick.

44)　A . . .　Right Side Spring Kick
　　　B . . .　Shrink Chest to Guard Against Leg

A retracts left leg, foot landing behind right foot(N-W). Weight shifts to left foot, torso turning swiftly to right rear(N). Right foot rises up in a Side Spring Kick to B's

Diag. H. 43.2

chest. Right arm swings out to rear, left arm bent in in front of chest. Gaze on B.

Having fended off A's left leg, B drops arms down in front of body. When A kicks with right leg, B swiftly shrinks chest, palms placed on pit of stomach to protect against A's kick. (Diag. H.44)

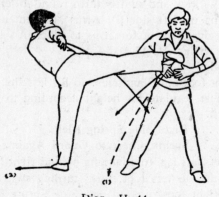

Diag. H. 44

Essentials:

A's three successive kicks should be fast, powerful and accurate.

45) **A ...** **Horse Stance with Downward Cross Palm**
      B ... **Horse Stance with Downward Cross Palm**

A's right foot lands at right side, toes pointing E. Left foot shifts a half step to left(W), toes pulled in, both legs bending to half squat to form Half Horse Stance. Right arm bends, forearm turning in, then thrusting down to right with straight arm and reverse palm, palm facing rear, crossing with B's right arm. Left palm is positioned by inside of right arm. Head turns right, gaze on B's arm.

B takes stride to right with right foot, both legs bending to half squat to form Horse Stance. Right forearm turns in, then thrusts down to right with straight arm and reverse palm, palm facing rear, crossing with A's right arm. Left palm is positioned by inside of right arm. Head turns right, gaze on A's arm. (Diag. H.45)

Essentials:

Both sides' movements must be completed together.

Diag. H. 45

46) A . . . Step Forward with Inward Kick
      B . . . Step Forward with Inward Kick

a) A's legs straighten up, torso turns left. Left foot rises up, toes turn out, left leg bends slightly. At same time, left palm swings out level to left side with Upright Palm. Right palm turns to fist and is withdrawn to waist. Gaze on left palm.

B's movements are same as A. (Diag. H. 46.1)

Diag. H. 46.1

b) A carries straight on. Pivoting on left foot, he swings right foot up in Inward Kick with sole turned in, left palm then slapping right sole. Right fist remains at waist. Gaze on right foot.

B's movements are same as A. (Diag. H. 46.2)
Essentials:

Both sides should turn and kick together, the slaps accurate, crisp and clear.

47) A . . . Bow Stance with Twin Palm Chops
      B . . . Bow Stance with Twin Palm Chops

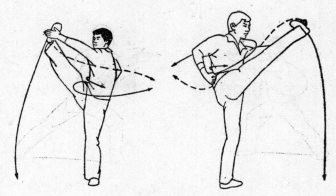

Diag. H. 46.2

A completes kick and turn, facing B (E). Right foot
lands to rear(W), leg straight, left leg bending to half
squat to form Left Bow Stance. At same time, both palms
swing out level from sides to meet, palms up, fingers
forward. Gaze on palms.

B completes kick and, pivoting on ball of left foot,
turns round to rear to face A(W). Right foot lands to
rear(E), leg straight, left leg bending to half squat to form
Left Bow Stance. Arms do same as A. Gaze on palms.
(Diag. H. 47)

Essentials:

Both sides' movements must be together. When right
leg lands to rear, heel stamps down forcefully, leg suddenly straightening.

48) A . . . Collect Hands to Attention
     B . . . Collect Hands to Attention

A shifts weight to rear, torso turning right, left foot
withdrawn to beside right to form Attention Stance. At
same time, both arms bend, separating to swing down and

399

Diag. H. 47

back past waist, then up and forward, forearms turning in, finally brought back together, bent in front of chest. Left palm turns to fist, in front of left chest, palm down. Right palm is above left forearm, palm facing left, fingers up. Head turns left. Gaze on B.

B's movements are same as A. (Diag. H.48)

Diag. H. 48

Essentials:

Both sides' movements must be together. A comes to attention facing S-E, B facing N-W. Torsos should twist left, keeping erect. Each should glare at the other.

49) A ... Return to Starting Posture
B ... Return to Starting Posture

A's left fist turns to palm, arms dropping by sides. Torso turns right so body faces S, as in Starting Position. Head turns left, gaze on B.

B's movements are same as A, but he faces N. (Diag. H.49)

Essentials:

Closing movement must be clean and simultaneous, both sides maintaining alert spirit.

Diag. H. 49

ILLUSTRATIONS OF VARIOUS TYPES OF THE BROADSWORD

Over the centuries a great many different weapons were developed in China. Here is a selection of some twenty or more varieties of long- and sshort-handled broadswords for your reference.

1) Long-handled Broadswords:
    i)   Sickle-hook Broadsword
    ii)   Three-pointed Twin-bladed Broadsword
    iii)   Elephant Trunk Broadsword
    iv)   Three-ring Broadsword
    v)   Pen Broadsword
    vi)   Phoenix-beak Broadsword
    vii)   Wide-bladed Medium Broadsword
    viii)   Eyebrow-pointed Broadsword
    ix)   Halberd
    x)   Moon-concealing Broadsword
    xi)   Crooked Broadsword
    xii)   Canine Broadsword

2) Short-handled Broadswords:
    xiii)   Single Broadsword
    xiv)   Japanese Broadsword
    xv)   Machete
    xvi)   Big-ring Broadsword
    xvii)   Waist Broadsword
    xviii)   Executioner's Broadsword
    xix)   Cavalry Broadsword
    xx)   Twin Broadswords
    xxi)   Ornamental Dagger
    xxii)   Daggers
    xxiii)   Flying Daggers

About the Author

Xie Zhikui, a Beijing native born in 1930, studied martial arts with his uncle from an early age. As a young man he placed himself under the tutelage of Song Dequan, Beijing's famous master of the Eight Trigrams and Flower styles of boxing. Master Song was accomplished at devising intricate patterns of striking movements, and he was skilled at quarterstaff. His strength in both hard and soft styles, his ability to lie asleep in a full split, and his ability to break rocks with his hands had brought him renown in martial arts circles. At the age of eighty Master Song could still jump onto a table and land in a headstand. The author, on commencing his apprenticeship, was the youngest and last of Master Song's pupils, or what was called the "gate-closing disciple." Master Song demanded a great deal of his pupils, often rousing them in the night to practise under the stars. Each day at noon he made them stand on posts to develop their balance, even in the heat of summer and the depths of winter. Their scheduled practice routines continued all year, with no interruptions for inclement weather. Now, though in his sixties, the author retains the physical conditioning of those years. His repertoire of skills is well-rounded, and his movements are precise, forceful and fluidly executed. The author is fond of playing martial roles in Peking opera, to which he brings a clever synthesis of theatrical technique and *kungfu*. His performances are remarkable for their emphasis on energy, force and spirit, and his accompanying hand

and eye movements convey a balance of spirit and feeling. Thus he satisfies the demand of martial arts for copresence of mind and body, and the fusion of inwardness with externality. He has made original contributions to techniques of eye, hand, body and foot movement, which in martial arts are of extreme subtlety. In boxing the author is versed in the Five Elements and Joined Rings styles. His preferred hand-held weapons are the broadsword, club, pike, spear, and that favoured weapon of monks, the crescent staff. His uniquely personal style has earned him a national first prize in martial arts.

Throughout his involvement with martial arts, he has sought out many teachers and colleagues to learn the following boxing styles: Flower, *Fanziquan,* Up-from-the-Ground, Monkey, Body and Will, *Taijiquan,* and Eight Trigrams. He is also versed in sparring unarmed or with weapons, in combat routines and in breath control *(Qigong).*

Beginning in the fifties, the author was a frequent prize-winner in municipal and national contests. In 1959 he captained the Beijing Martial Arts Team in the First National Games, assisted by coaches Zhang Wenguang and Chang Zhenfang, with the technical assistance of Li Tianji, Wu Binlou and Li Jingwu.

Since concluding his own career as an athlete, the author has groomed a great number of students as a professor of martial arts for over twenty years at the Beijing Physical Culture Teachers College. He continues to act as coach or instructor for martial arts classes at various universities, schools, martial arts centres and foreign embassies. He also frequently joins in compiling martial arts textbooks, producng educational films, and formulating sparring and combat rules for the State Physical Culture and

Sports Commission.

Xie Zhikui also serves as vice-chairman of the Beijing East District Martial Arts Association; chief referee and executive committee member of Beijing Municipal Martial Arts Association; and member of Theoretical and Scientific Research Committee, China Martial Arts Association. He is frequently named referee or chief referee in municipal and national contests.

The model for the photographs in the book is the author's son Xie Jun, aged 27. An early learner at his father's knee, he was admitted at fourteen to the China Coal Miners' Art Troupe, in which he performs classical Chinese dance. Upon perfecting his "Drunken Sword" dance, in 1982 he accompanied the cast of the dance drama "Rain of Flowers on the Silk Road" on a tour to the United States and Canada.

中国单刀
——从基本技术到表演
套路的教学全书
谢志奎 编著
特约编辑：曾维祺

*

外文出版社出版
（中国北京百万庄路24号）
邮政编码 100037
外文印刷厂印刷
中国国际图书贸易总公司发行
（中国北京車公庄西路21號）
北京邮政信箱第399号邮政编码100044
1990年（34开）第一版
（英）
00905
7-119-00830-7/G·19(外)
7-E- 2390 P